Ramblings of a
Rambler

Published under licence by Brown Dog Books and
The Self-Publishing Partnership, 7 Green Park Station, Bath BA1 1JB

www.selfpublishingpartnership.co.uk

ISBN printed book: 978-1-83952-069-3

Cover design and illustrations by Andrew Prescott
Internal design by Andrew Easton

Printed and bound in the UK

This book is printed on FSC certified paper

MIX
Paper from
responsible sources
FSC
www.fsc.org
FSC® C013604

Ramblings of a
Rambler

John Oldcorn's Thames Walk, 1999 to 2008

(part travelogue, part wildlife commentary,
certainly a walking guide but without doubt,
mainly a 9-year pub crawl)

John Oldcorn

BROWN
DOG
BOOKS

Acknowledgements/Disclaimers:

- Dad used the National Trail Guide by David Sharp, 1996 edition, to plot his route along the Thames

- The pub reviews that appear in this book are taken from the internet, often from the website of the pub

- Any factual inaccuracies. Too bad, he's dead and we have already spent the inheritance so there's no point suing us

- Some of the photos are a load of crap, but that's what dad captured (often on an analogue camera – you will need to ask your parents about that kids…) and we wouldn't want to change a thing about them (there's a classic in Chapter 17 folks)!

Introduction

In 1999, my dad set out to walk the Thames, from the East End of London to the Thames Head, at Kemble in the Cotswolds.

Dad was not a Lycra warrior. His plan was to walk the Thames by a series of separate walks, when he could fit them in, taking in all that nature and the modern world might throw at him.

He didn't set out to break any records, unless there is a record for having at least two pints in every pub along the Thames. In fact he didn't even finish the damn walk, as he had to give up 800 yards short of the finish line, but what he did create was this set of notes that document his adventures en route. I couldn't find the notes that he made during a couple of sections but fortunately most were knocking about his study.

If you knew my dad, this little book will transport you straight back to the pub that you used to sit and drink with him in, where you would have sat listening for hours to his silly stories, most of which seemed quite unbelievable, but were of course true. If you didn't know Dad in that environment, perhaps because you are one of his grandchildren and drinking IPA with him at five years old would have been inappropriate, it will tell you a little bit about your Grandpa John.

Younger readers might wince, a little, at some of the views expressed in this book. So please, remember two things: (1) times change. (2) Dad wouldn't give a toss…

…so I haven't changed it…too much!

Phillip Oldcorn, 3rd August 2019

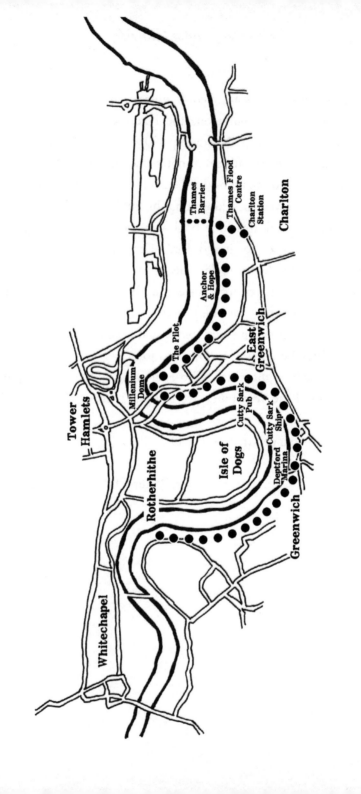

1.
The East End – Charlton to Rotherhithe

Tuesday 18 May 1999

It's 10.00 am and I'm leaving High Wycombe station.

I've bought a through ticket to Charlton. That ticket cost me £39.60, which isn't a bad deal. Takes me all the way there and all the way back, apart from the little bit that I'm going to do on my feet!

I bought a copy of *The Guardian* for 45p.

It is now 12.05…almost two hours since I left High Wycombe and I've made the journey from High Wycombe to Marylebone, across London on the Bakerloo line to Charing Cross and then out on the train to Charlton station. So I'm already pretty bloody knackered and I've not yet started the Thames Walk.

At Charlton station a young chap in a wheelchair got out of the train and headed towards some steps. There were about 20 steps. I thought, "How the hell is he going to get up those steps in a wheelchair?"

Well, when he got to them, he threw himself out of his chair onto the ground and dragged himself and his chair to the first step. He then threw his chair onto the second step and dragged himself up to meet it. He then repeated this performance. I went over and said I would carry his chair up the steps and leave him to drag himself after me. He was very grateful. This wheelchair, which had looked as light as a feather when he was throwing it around, turned out to weigh a bloody ton. I nearly didn't make it up the stairs.

The moral to this story is that next time I see a lad in a wheelchair, he can damn well carry it himself.

I am sitting here on a bench looking at the Thames Barrier for the first time. It's queer but I feel an ownership with this structure. In my capacity as a civil servant for the Ministry of Agriculture, Fisheries and Food, I was once responsible for controlling the funds that built it. It has ten separate movable gates and is the world's second-largest movable flood barrier.

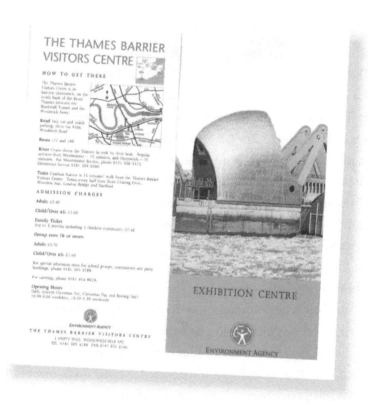

As I sit here, I contemplate how typical it is of England, that someone thought it appropriate to fly the Thames Water flag proudly from the top and someone else, I assume (who couldn't give a bugger), has allowed it to deteriorate to a shredded nonsense. How could you see that each day and not feel it necessary either to replace it or to abandon the flag idea?

Imagine the passengers on the visiting cruises looking at that and saying, "Thames Water! Never heard of them, but they must be a pretty shredded organisation to fly a flag like that!" Come to think of it, they would probably say, "'Tha Wat'…what on earth does that mean?"

It looks like a pair of torn knickers up there.

Well enough of this, I'm about to go in and see what there is to see in the Exhibition Centre…

…and there was a great deal in there. It was definitely worth the visit. There was a film show about the Thames and why a barrier was needed to prevent flooding. There was a video showing how the barrier was constructed and there were working models of it.

The cinema seats about a hundred but I was the only one there. They ran the film especially for me and one of the wrinkled old retainers came over and introduced himself to me. He accompanied me round explaining all there was to see: most of it didn't actually need explanation. He was very enthusiastic and I am always cheered by people who obviously enjoy what they are doing. I hadn't the heart to tell him to get the shredded knickers off the line.

So I've left there now and I've actually started the walk. I stopped off at the "Anchor and Hope"* – (not the "Hope and Anchor" interestingly). This was the first opportunity to break my resolve not to stop at every pub on the way, and I took it. It was "Toby" bitter and it was well worth breaking my resolve for! It was wonderful and now I feel so much better,

so much younger and my stride even now, as I speak, is lengthening.
*this pub has since been demolished

The scenery along here is pretty dismal. Gravel workings and stone washing. There are piles and piles of crap. Piles on top of piles. There's an army of JCBs building up the piles. Where does all this come from?

No wonder the video said that this corner of England is sinking! It wouldn't sink if they took away some of this bloody rubbish. We might not have needed the barrier if they had just removed the rubbish. Why not take it to France and sink France? God, there is a place here with piles and piles of huge lumps of concrete. What would you want to store concrete for? The scene here is of complete devastation. There are conveyors shifting concrete, there are silos of smashed-up concrete. What a godforsaken hole this is.

There is a splendid view here of the Dome. The new Millennium Dome, surrounded by ongoing work.

I've now got as far as Greenwich, west of the Dome. Walking that area was difficult, because all of the roads are new. They seem to have ripped out everything that was there and started again. It seems odd that the access to all this is just one road and because it's a peninsula you have to come out the way you go in. Where I am now is not very nice. The area is dull and uninteresting and it's like walking through a scrapyard. I photographed an area which a local firm has provided for the enjoyment of the people of Greenwich and a photo of the sponsor's sign. I have seldom seen such a dump…

Interestingly, when I was walking around Greenwich I did find the "Pilot" pub which features in my walking guide and I couldn't resist popping in for one: hard to believe but there you go.

It's in the middle of the construction site. I talked to the girl behind the bar and she said that it had been like that for some months and regulars have to ring up to check where the car park is since it changes almost every day. Interesting, too, that the beer in there was £2.10 a pint, whereas the pint half a mile away at the "Hope" was only £1.80. Obviously the nearer you get to London, the more you pay for your beer. It will be interesting to record, as I continue on this wander, how the price of the amber nectar doth change.

I have this notion that the landlord here used to shout, "Have you no homes to go to?" when he wanted to close the pub. He stopped when everyone called back, "No, they've knocked the buggers down!"

The Pilot, Greenwich

The Pilot is the epitome of modern hospitality. But the pub actually dates back more than 200 years, built in the early 1800s to serve the local coal workers.

A painted stone tablet on the wall of the pub reads "CEYLON PLACE New East Greenwich 1801" – dating The Pilot as probably the oldest surviving building on the Greenwich Peninsula.

Next to the pub is a row of eight cottages that were constructed for workers at the adjacent tidal mill and chemical works. They are "a rare survival of late Georgian artisan housing" and are Grade II listed for their protection.

The cottages are noted for another reason, too – they were used as the backdrop to Blur's 'Parklife' music video! The pub itself also features in the video, grabbing a little slice of 90s Britpop glory!

Just dropped another clanger. I stopped to talk to two young lads working on the riverbank. One had a red eye.

I said, as you do, "Your missus been knocking you around, then?" He said, "No actually it's a birthmark." Shit! I told him he looked very distinctive, but it was a bollock all the same.

I've taken a photo of a boat that John Holland and I could buy. It wants a little bit doing up, but with a little bit of effort and the odd weekend, I think that we could make it shipshape. It's moored up to a very shabby structure, made of scaffolding and empty containers. A real mess!

Next door there is a little jetty, where I imagine they bring tourists just to see what a heap England can be, if you leave it to the devices of some people. The contrast between this area and the opposite bank of the river is very marked.

I assume that the other bank was in this condition once and has been rejuvenated. Hopefully this area will be like that one day but it's hard to imagine right now. Anyway, the graffiti artists are cheering things up. Some of it looks quite competent, actually.

I stopped at "The Cutty Sark" pub for a pint. Well, you owe it to the kids. It's as I thought. The beer in there was £2.20. By the time I get to Tower Bridge it's going to be £10.00 a pint! But it was a wonderful old pub. A listed building. Built in 1695, it has a tremendously attractive staircase, rising from the centre as soon as you walk into the place.

The Cutty Sark

Sat on the banks of the Thames at Ballast Quay, The Cutty Sark has welcomed guests for over two hundred years.

We are proud to be part of this long tradition of serving the highest-quality British produce, accompanied by fine wines from around the world and great real ales. We are about premium seasonal British pub food providing the best fresh fish dishes you'll find in Greenwich.

We are located along the Thames Path, the nearest train stations are: Maze Hill station – 7-min walk (0.4 miles) Cutty Sark DLR station – 10-min walk (0.6 miles)

I presented myself at the Cutty Sark, hoping to have a look around this tourist attraction. I was joined by some Americans and some French people. It's a pleasant Tuesday night and it's 4.30pm. We were all to be disappointed. The attraction had closed for the day. The American said, as he walked away, "Thank you, England. That's so typical." I must say I had to agree with him. I did point out to the guys who turned us away that the notice on the noticeboards was so badly spelt that it was laughable.

I've just noticed another sign indicating that discount vouchers have to be presented at the commencement of the transaction. 'Vouchers' is spelt with an apostrophe s! These people have no bloody idea.

The path leaves the river for quite some distance here and I have to wander through streets and roads and wasteland. None of this is very attractive. This has been the worst section of the walk so far. I'm now walking along Deptford Walk and I'm glad to see the river again. Francis Drake set sail from here aboard the *Golden Hind* in 1577, on his first round-the-world expedition. 200 years later, in 1768, Captain Cook left Deptford in the *Endeavour* to discover Australia.

I'm also getting tired now and it is 17.45. I need to think about getting back to Marylebone.

There's a thing here that I am looking at. It's like a miniature scaffold that you might sit a globe in. There's a note that says it is art on the waterfront and it's called "circumsphere" by Chris Marsh and Steven Lewis. It apparently shows the route that Sir Francis Drake took when he circumnavigated the world in 1581. It's not really attractive and seems pretty pointless. Someone has written across it in black felt pen: "An't dis a load of balls". He or she actually got the two "l's" in balls which I thought was commendable.

This is a nice stretch, walking along the South Bank, looking over the river to Canary Wharf, past Deptford Marina, very pleasant. 6 o'clock in the evening and not a soul in sight. I must say that the north bank from here looks very attractive. There are lots of little piers here to negotiate. All this seems new. Probably old warehouses that have been yuppified. It all looks rather nice. This one here – "Greenland Pier" – is enormous.

Here is some more riverside art. A piece of air ducting bent and twisted either by design or by accident – it's not clear which. The finished product is unrecognisable and is titled "Curly Quieu" by William Pie. Well, William, you must have been stoned out of your brain when you came up with that. It really is pointless. "A load of balls", others may think.

I have left the walk. Decided to call it a day and look for a tube station and where do you find information about such things? Well, you find it in a pub called "The Ship York". What a great pub – I'm not sure just where it is. I would never find it again.*

What a good crack. I had three pints with some super chaps. One was a History lecturer who told me that he had lots of papers to mark and books to review this evening. I asked him who taught English around here. I mentioned the Cutty Sark notices. He said that if he saw the word "cannot" spelt as one word like that, he would just put a pencil through it! I said, "But it is correct as one word." He said, "No, you are wrong." I rested my case.

The Ship York was in Rotherhithe Street SE16 5LJ, and Dad was correct, he wouldn't find it again as it closed in November 2014 and was then knocked down for flats.

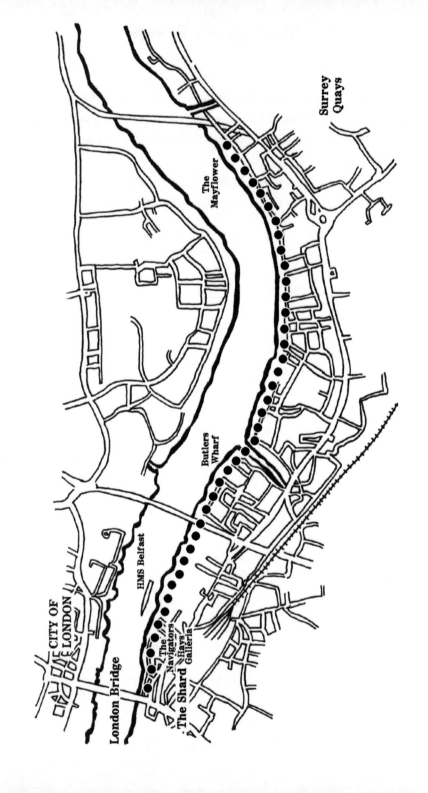

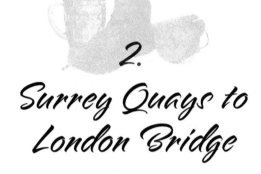

2.
Surrey Quays to London Bridge

It is 15 June, Tuesday, 1999. Simon's birthday.
Today I went to Amersham for a stress test. I've been having strange discomfort in my chest. Nothing showed up on the test.

I am at Surrey Quays, where I left the walk last time.

I walked to London Bridge. Not a very interesting walk. Much of the time the walk takes you through backstreets away from the river. Couple of nice pubs enticed me in. One called "The Mayflower" claimed (along with lots of other pubs) that the captain of the *Mayflower*, Captain Christopher Jones, was a regular there before he set off with the Pilgrim Fathers. I'm surprised he ever got out of the Thames because, if he drank in half the pubs that claim his former custom, he must have been three parts pissed most of the time. I had a pint and took a look at the view. There was nothing historic about it. In fact, I could see nothing older than about ten years. Still they had got the price of a pint out of me.

www.mayflowerpub.co.uk

In July 1620, the Mayflower ship took on-board 65 passengers from its London home port of Rotherhithe on the River Thames. Rumour has it that Captain Christopher Jones cunningly moored here to avoid paying taxes further down the river. The Mayflower journeyed onwards to Southampton for supplies and to rendezvous with the Speedwell but after many delays, false starts and a devastating leak, the Speedwell's journey with the Mayflower was abandoned. On 6 September 1620, Captain Jones, along with 102 passengers and approximately 30 crew members, set sail from Plymouth on what William Bradford described as "a prosperous wind".

After sighting land on 11 November 1620, strong winter seas forced the Rotherhithe captain to anchor at Cape Cod, much further north than the original destination of Virginia. To establish legal order in their new homeland the settlers agreed, whilst on-board, to write and sign "The Mayflower Compact", the first written framework of government in what is now the United States.

Captain Jones later returned to London on the Mayflower, arriving at the home port of Rotherhithe on 6 May 1621. He died less than a year later and was buried at St Mary's church in Rotherhithe, close to the mooring point of the Mayflower where she was laid to rest in the Thames, no longer useful as a ship. A commemorative plaque to the voyage of the Mayflower now adorns the side of St Mary's church and a memorial statue, dedicated to the memory of Captain Christopher Jones, sits in the churchyard.

WHY DOES THE MAYFLOWER PUB SELL STAMPS?

Back in the 1800s, seafarers docking at Rotherhithe with little time to spare were able to order a pint and a postage stamp here at The Mayflower (formerly The Spread Eagle). We are still the only pub licensed to sell US & UK postage stamps – just ask at the bar!

In fact, throughout the entire walk today, I have seen nothing along the track that wasn't new, except for one or two places where old riverside warehouses have been made into apartments.

The outer original structure is still intact but they are very modern apartments and they look very nice indeed. I couldn't quite work out why in some cases the old warehouses seem to have been totally demolished, and in others there seems to have been a compulsion on the developer to maintain the original outer fabric and convert the inside. I'm glad that they did.

An interesting walk. A development called the "Galleria" was nice.*

It was obviously a little dock where boats would be loaded and unloaded. The little dock had been preserved and residential properties with shops and a restaurant and a modern sculpture called "The Navigator" had been installed. All in all, very impressive.

*Hays Galleria

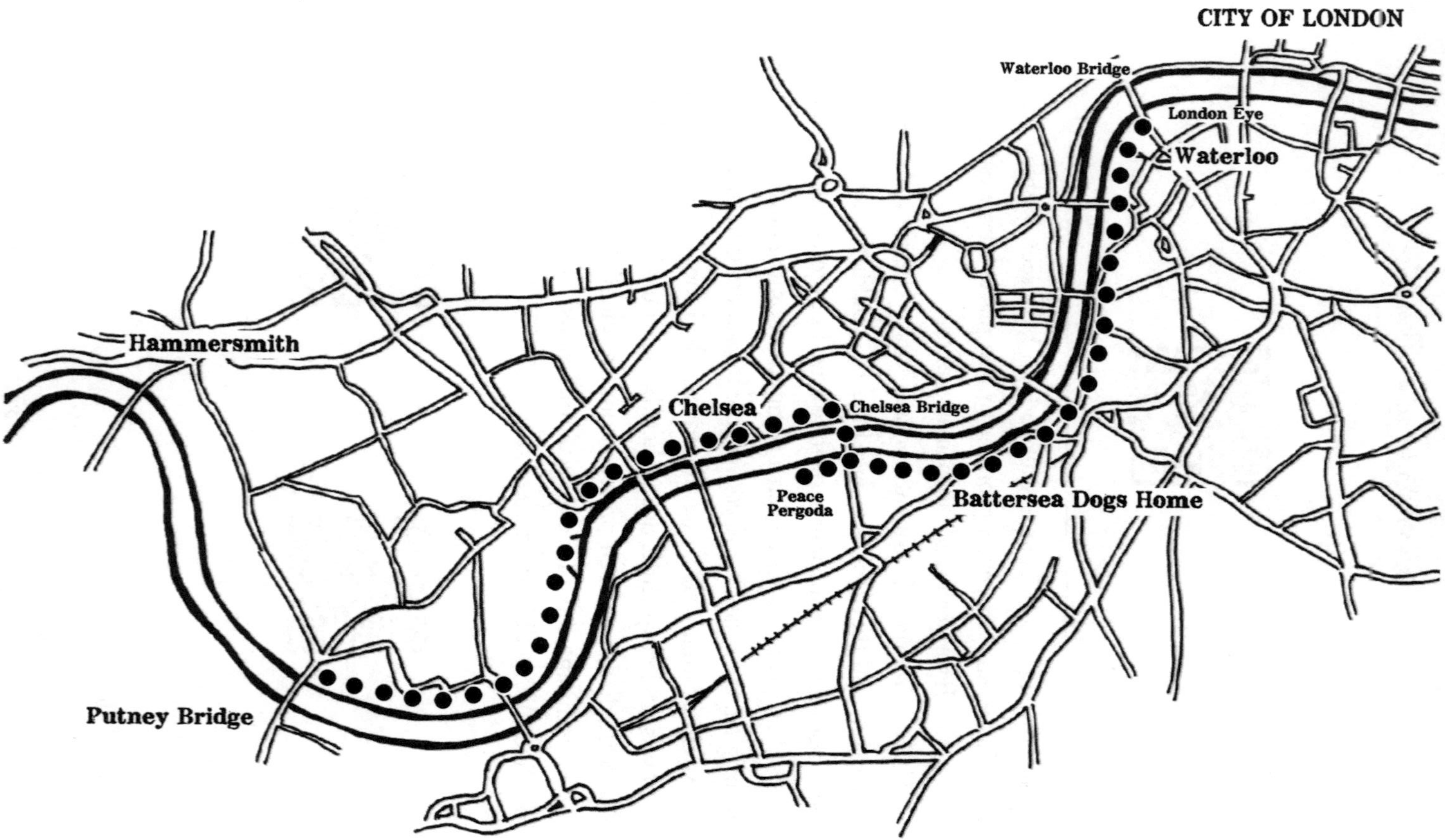

CITY OF LONDON

Waterloo Bridge

London Eye

Waterloo

Chelsea Bridge

Battersea Dogs Home

Chelsea

Peace Pergoda

Hammersmith

Putney Bridge

3
Waterloo to Putney Bridge Monday, 22 May, the year 2000.

The Millennium Year. And here I am. I've begun again, or I'm hoping to begin to add some miles to the Thames Walk. I haven't been able to get to it for various reasons. None of which would bear examination. But there you go!

I'm in my new camper van, for which I paid £6,000 in September. And here I am now on this pleasant May evening at Laleham campsite.

It's a little bit chilly but the sun is shining, and it's 8 o'clock and I'm in shorts and "T" shirt, so that can't be bad. And I'm cooking on the stove in the van, sweet and sour pork with pasta shells. That's a very odd mix, I know, but it just seemed to me that pasta shells would be easier to do than anything else tonight.

OK, I've finished my meal now. I'm glad I did the pasta shells because the sweet and sour pork was not that good.

The pork was bought at British Home Stores* in Staines. I didn't even know that BHS sold food, but when I went in there looking for a light for the van, there was some food on sale and I bought some pork, cubed pork, and a sweet and sour sauce mix. The pork was absolutely tasteless. It didn't taste of anything, least alone pork. The sweet and sour sauce was… sweet and sour. But there you go. In life you find these things out and you make these mental notes:

"Don't buy pork at BHS because whoever is producing it for them is feeding his pigs on water."

So I am now sitting in the van, with a glass of red wine and I'm looking around at this campsite which needs some explanation, because it is very odd. Because when I phoned, thinking that at this time of year this campsite would be reasonably free, I was surprised that the lady said she could only accommodate me for two nights.

Now that I have got here the situation seems even more puzzling. Because the site seems to be settled with what appears to be static tents. All more or less 12' x 12'.

All, or more or less all of them, have long grass growing around them. All are scruffy, scruffy, scruffy. There isn't a pleasant-looking tent on the site. All are very scruffy. If it was my campsite I would say, "Shift your scruffy tents and let's brighten the place up."

I assume that these tents are either Eurocamp tents (one has got flags all around it) or are owned by private people who have a permanent pitch here, which explains why it might be difficult from time to time to get in. If that's the case I think that it's worth making a point about this because this is one of the few camps along the Thames Walk. If it's going to be permanently occupied by these scruffy tents, I think that is a policy which ought to be bloody changed really. That's not what campsites are about. All of these scruffy tents have enormous gas bottles outside, and all of them have three gas bottles – and these are enormous gas bottles.

Historical note: younger viewers, British Home Stores was a major High Street department store, until it controversially went bust in 2017. Perhaps because the food was a load of crap?

It is Tuesday, 23 May 2000. I have walked from the campsite into Laleham, got a bus there (eventually) to Staines where I got a train into Waterloo, and I set off walking from Waterloo along the South Bank. I was much taken, much impressed in fact, by what's called the new "London Eye" – which is a great, big wheel in which people sit in gondolas and they're taken up a huge height.

There was a huge queue, so I didn't bother queuing to go in, because I had other things to do. At the Eye, I bumped into Don and Min Dickerson from the rugby club. They had also been very impressed. So that's one thing I must do, so I went to the ticket office and got details of how to get tickets.

Made my way further along the Embankment. It's a nice walk. Took some pictures of Battersea Power Station and Vauxhall Bridge. Vauxhall Bridge is an attractive bridge. I then went into Battersea Dogs & Cats Home. Spent an interesting three-quarters of an hour looking at the caged dogs there, or kennelled dogs I suppose is a better expression. It advises everyone not to put your fingers through the door. On every door there is a brief description of the dog and what the new owner could expect of it. On some of them, the notice says: "requires an owner with no fingers".

Somebody who has nothing left to lose, in other words. Some of them look quite vicious. Whether that is caused by the situation that they are in, I don't know. I did notice that some have been there for an awfully long time and one wonders, "Do they keep them forever?" I don't know.

The walk takes you away from the river at this stage, through a rather run-down area. I crossed the river on Chelsea Bridge and walked along what I think is called the Chelsea Reach. There are houseboats here. It looks like people live on them. I noticed that one was for sale. And so onwards and upwards through Battersea Park, which is very pretty. There's the "London Peace Pagoda" in there, which is very attractive – and on to Putney Bridge.

The Peace Pagoda in Battersea Park

I'd had enough by then, so I decided to get a train back to Staines. This is where my arrangements went haywire.

I thought that Putney was mainline. It wasn't. I had to catch a train to somewhere! Then change to come back down to Clapham Common. I got a train there and – of course – the next station we stopped at was Putney.

All that messing about was for nothing. I was on a stopping train. It didn't stop at Bristol Parkway, but that was probably only one of very few stations it missed!

I got to Staines at 615 and debated whether to eat out or cook. I thought, "Well, you're supposed to be testing this van out," so I decided to cook. I went to Sainsbury's to buy some goodies and got back to the station to find that the bus had gone at 1850, not 1900. There wasn't another until 2050.

So what do you do? Well – if you haven't had a pint all day you have a pint. So I found a pub and had three and got a taxi back to the site. I knocked up a very pleasant meal. Had a glass or two of wine and retired.

The Star

Nice little pub, lots of live music & sport. The owners advertise themselves as "The Drinking Consultants", so they need to be patronised.

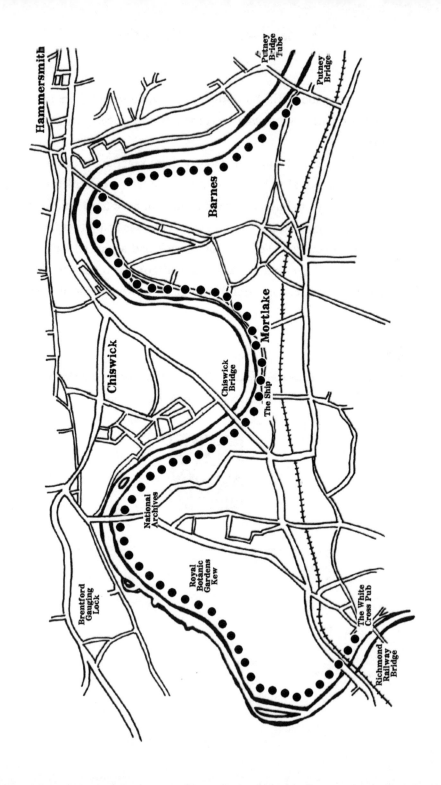

4.
Putney to Richmond, Teddington, then back to Twickenham!
(Aka The "No Bridges" Incident)

It is Wednesday 24 May 2000 and I'm walking again. I've just passed under Kew Bridge (more of that later). I've just seen a big bird. Black. Six-foot wingspan. Yellow beak. White blaze behind its eye. Never seen one before, I don't think. It dived into the water and came up with an eel, probably more than a foot long. It swam up the river a little way then swallowed the damn thing whole. I don't believe it. It took some getting down, I'll tell you.

It has just started raining so I've put my coat on. It has been much better today than yesterday, when it rained all day long. Much nicer walking day today.

I've walked from Putney Bridge past Barnes under Chiswick Bridge. Past the breweries: Mortlake Brewery and Fuller's. To both of whom I paused to pay dutiful homage. Stopped at the "Ship" (in Mortlake), on the bank of the river and had just the one pint. Well, I owe it to the kids, don't I? Strange, though, that, even though it was within spitting distance of the Fuller's Brewery, it was a Courage pub.

The Ship

Built in 1781, The Ship is without doubt most famous for its location on the finishing line of the Oxford/Cambridge Boat Race. This ex-Taylor Walker pub now has external Greene King branding. Located at the end of Ship Lane off the Lower Richmond Road in Mortlake, to the rear of what was the old Watneys Brewery, The Ship is set back off the river.

The Ship in Mortlake is a gorgeous riverside pub and is as picturesque as the scenery. A quintessentially English pub, you can enjoy the timber floors, an open fire, beer garden and the best of British pub food and drink.

On the road from Putney to Barnes, which is a pleasant path by the riverside, you could be miles from anywhere along parts of it. This guy was walking towards me; he stopped me and asked, "Is there a bridge down here?" I said, "No."

He said, "No bridges?" I said, "No. You'll not find a bridge in London. You would be better to turn around. Go the other way. Walk out to Hampton Court. I've been there early in the morning when the commuters arrive. They go to an assembly point on the South Bank where they strip off. They put all their clothes and belongings in plastic bags, which are provided, and swim across to their offices. There are drying rooms on the other bank. Everyone goes in bare, dries off, gets dressed and goes on to a nice day at the office, refreshed. There's no segregation but no one minds, there would be no point. They all come in on the same train. In fact, if you had a little boat you could make a small fortune, especially on a cold day. And especially if you got a pitch opposite the House of Commons. One of these days someone will build a bridge from the south bank to the north and they will make a fortune."

He asked, "How far are you walking?" I said, "To Oxford" – he looked at me incredulously. Then he pointed up the river and said, "It's that way, I think."

Anyway, I'm glad he stopped me, otherwise I might not have stopped at The Ship. If he hadn't, I might not have done that.

I've stopped now to take a photograph of the start of the Grand Union Canal at Brentford. This is a historic place. It is where loads and loads of commodities were brought down on barges and off-shipped here, onto Thames barges, to go down to the coast. Must have been a busy, busy place at that time.

I've taken another photograph at almost the same spot because it just struck me that you can still find a scene like that, almost in the heart of London, certainly in the heart of the suburbs of London. You would think that you were miles away.

I have now got to Richmond. I've just taken a photo of Richmond railway bridge, just as Concorde was flying over. I hope that it shows up on the picture.

Richmond Bridge with Concorde just visible in the background

I've also taken a photo upriver, towards Twickenham Bridge, a very pleasant stone-built bridge with Richmond Hill in the background. I'm leaving the walk here today at Young's White Cross pub.

The White Cross, Richmond

Serving Young's fine ales since 1869, the pub dates back to 1780 and was originally called The Watermans Arms.

It was rebuilt in 1838, and changed its name to The White Cross in 1840. The landlord at the time was Samuel Cross which may explain the name change. The pub is built on the site of the observant Franciscan friary which was dissolved by Henry VIII in 1534, but there may be some remains of the friary incorporated within our extensive cellars. Also unique to The White

Cross is our cosy fireplace which is situated underneath a window and one of only a tiny number of which are still used in this country.

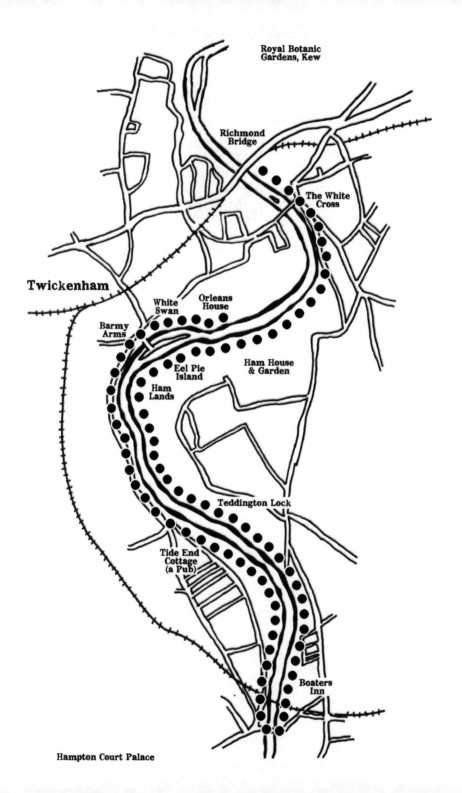

Royal Botanic
Gardens, Kew

Richmond
Bridge

The White
Cross

Twickenham

Orleans
House

White
Swan

Barmy
Arms

Eel Pie
Island

Ham House
& Garden

Ham
Lands

Teddington Lock

Tide End
Cottage
(a Pub)

Boaters
Inn

Hampton Court Palace

5.
Richmond to Kingston & Twickenham

I have left Richmond now and made my way down the south bank to Teddington and I've sat down on a picnic table outside The Boaters Inn at Kingston.

The Boaters Kingston

The Boaters is a lovely riverside pub situated in Canbury Gardens, just a ten-minute walk away from Central Kingston. We feature a riverside beer garden that backs on to a park and a quiet sunset balcony.

I'm going to have my packed lunch and treat myself to a pint. Two minutes to one. I don't believe it. It must be a damn unlucky day for fish. I've just seen another guy catch one. This was all of six inches long. He said to his mate that it was a roach. He got it off the hook and threw it into a keepnet.

Now here's another funny thing. Not only has he dragged it out of the water and let it dangle on the end of a rope with a piece of iron through its gob, but he's also going to torture it for the rest of the afternoon by penning it into his net. Then at the end of the day he will empty his keepnet into the river. What's the bloody point of that, then?!

I feel like leaping into the river and splashing about and shouting, "Fish – keep away from this bank. Stay in the middle. Keep away from these bloody berks!"

I've photographed the three locks at Teddington. This, I think, is where the tidal section of the river starts. The biggest of these locks is called the Barge Lock and it's 650 feet long and can fit a steam tug and six river barges. It's huge. During the war, the flotilla of little ships, from along the Thames, assembled here before setting off for Dunkirk. HQ for this operation was set up in The Tide End pub (the pub is still there but now called The Tide End Cottage) beside the lock.

The Tide End Cottage pub is situated 50 yards from the bank of the River Thames. The pub dates back to 1820. It was near this pub on the River Thames at Tough's boat yard that 100 "small ships" were assembled prior to their perilous passage across the English Channel to assist in the Dunkirk evacuation in May 1940. The old pub sign (now replaced) depicted the evacuation of the BEF under German fire. The pub has a deceptively small frontage but it goes back a long way. It has

recently been completely refurbished internally and reopened in May 2015.

I've just walked through an area called "Ham Lands," a very wild area kept that way to provide a space for wildlife. I am now crossing to the other bank on a small ferry and I'm heading back on the north bank in the direction that I've just come to visit Twickenham. I intend to find the Barmy Arms – well, I owe it to the kids to do that.

The Barmy Arms isn't barmy anymore. There's nothing barmy about it. It's just become another also-ran pub. The theme now is Twickenham with rugby tickets up behind the bar. Shame really!*

Barmy Arms, Twickenham

The Barmy Arms is a beautiful river-front pub situated in the old part of Twickenham.

Just a 20-minute walk from Twickenham Stadium, open from 10 am on match days. With a large, covered patio area overlooking the Thames and Eel Pie Island, join us after the game for our great after-rugby parties.

---

* Fortunately the pub has recovered since. Dad took me to the Barmy Arms on my first visit to Twickenham to watch Gosforth in the final of the John Player Cup in May 1981. My first experience of an away rugby match, a coach full of dads, pubs, hotel and all sorts of other things! The Barmy Arms is still a regular

haunt and always great fun.

I then had a pint at The White Swan just along the riverbank. I've had many a pre-match pint here. It has a huge beer garden/retail area at low tide but this shrinks as the tide comes in!

White Swan, Twickenham

The White Swan is a traditional free house right on the banks of the River Thames in Twickenham. The pub dates back to the 17th century. The pub is made up of two rooms, a terrace-balcony and a garden right on the riverbank. It's a very cosy pub in winter, especially when we light the fires. In summer we open the doors to the balcony and put up sunshades in the garden. Sometimes, at high tide, the garden is IN the river but never for long. Everyone who works here knows what it's like to wade through the water with a few plates or glasses in hand.

I then went into Orleans House to get out of a rain shower and there was an exhibition in the gallery of views from Richmond Hill, which has been a preserved view for 100 years. There were some splendid pictures. Some of them were 200 years old. The contemporary contribution was by a woman called Alchurch and she was exhibiting three photographs.

They were the ugliest, worst composed photos I have ever seen. Designed to show the worst aspects of Richmond Hill. I wonder what might motivate that view of such a lovely place? Her work will last until about next year.

That's it, that's the end of this section. I will now start again from Staines and resume walking upriver. I found a pub called The George in Staines. It's a Wetherspoons pub. Believe it or not, the Spitfire in there was £1.40 per pint. God bless you, Mr Wetherspoon.

The George Inn, Staines

From the 15th century at least, The George Inn stood on this site. It ceased trading in the late–18th century, and the building was demolished later in the 19th.

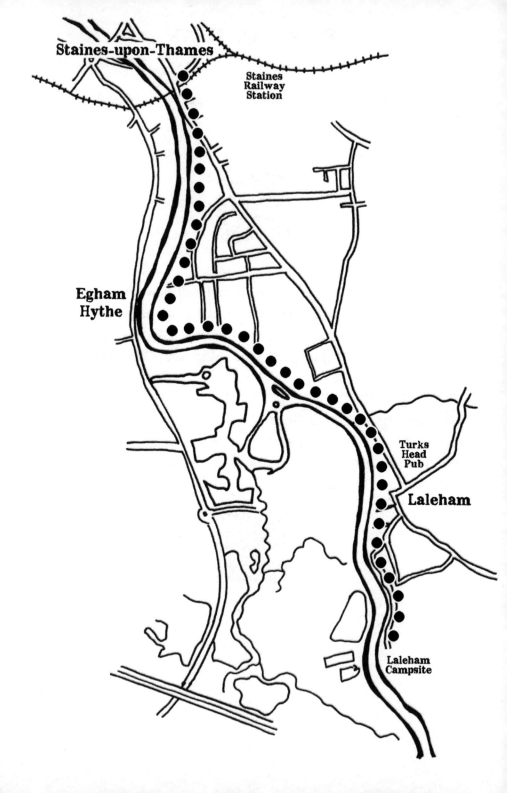

Staines-upon-Thames

Staines
Railway
Station

Egham
Hythe

Turks
Head
Pub

Laleham

Laleham
Campsite

6.
Laleham to Staines
Saturday 13 April 2002.

Unbelievably this is the first chance that I have had to get back to the Thames Walk. So here I am. I've just arrived at Laleham campsite. I don't think that I am very popular at the rugby club because I have left them on the final league game of the season, but I don't really care about that. I was ready for a break.

It's a spring day, the trees are just beginning to show their leaves. It's bright and sunny but there is an east wind, so it is a little bit cold but not too cold.

I have Poppy with me, because John and Norma Holland are off to Barbados tomorrow. I thought she would enjoy this adventure as much as me. She looks quite comfortable. It's 1530. I didn't get here until late because I went to the club to make sure that the bar was OK before I left. There is certainly time to have an hour's walk so I'm going to go with Poppy from the campsite at Laleham and incidentally, the campsite looks a lot better than it did last time I was here (see Chapter 3).

Poppy Holland and dad's camper van

All the grass has been cut, the tents don't look as if they have been abandoned. It really looks quite smart. There's a bit of activity, some kiddies are playing around the site.

My plan tomorrow is to walk from here, downriver, which is a reverse of what I have been doing so far. I have made that plan because it seems that public transport on Sundays is abysmal. So I can't go to Staines, by a non-existent bus service. But this evening, my plan is to walk upriver to Staines.

On the riverbank here are some pretty little shacks that people must live in. I see one is on stilts – probably to prevent flooding when the river is high. There are loads of pretty little places that people must live in. There's one here that I'm going to take a picture of. A strange boat. It looks like it has got a mast and it has something on the side that looks like some sort of a paddle, but it can't possibly be a paddle.

Strange boat....what's that paddle all about?

It's an absolutely beautiful evening. The wind has dropped, the willow trees are at their very best. Poppy is striding out in front of me. She looks like she's enjoying it. She's certainly enjoying every smell. There's a sign here that says "Wild Foul": Poppy just looked at it as if she were reading a menu.

There are some very lovely houses on this stretch. There are some damn ugly ones, too. I wonder how the planners can allow people to build houses that look as awful as the two that I have just passed. Just boxes.

I've just come across a house here and it has got a name on it,

"Mullagmore". The house is bounded by a yew hedge and there's a flower bed on the riverside. It's just there for people to see, because it can't be seen from the house. It's just done for the pleasure of people walking by. It's absolutely beautiful. I can see white campion, yellow campion. I can see forget-me-not, grape hyacinth, buxus, euonymus, choisya, pieris, aubretia, mahonia. There's juniper and loads of stuff that I can't recognise but the whole bed is full of colour and loveliness. Oh, and there are fawn bluebells and white rock. Thanks to whoever did this and takes care of it. It's all set off by this beautiful yew hedge, clipped to perfection. Oh look at the end here, that's bay, clipped to a cone shape. I can see a lovely clematis in the garden there. They must have a gardener, and loads of money!

Now, on the other hand, the house next door, gorgeous house, mock-Elizabethan, he's got a hawthorn hedge and bless him, he has dug up the soil underneath the hedge: it looks like good soil but he's got sweet bugger all growing in it.

We come to another monstrosity of a house, which someone must have thought looked good on paper. It's got an ugly decking at the back. God, it looks awful.

Well, here I am at Staines.

Now I'm almost back at the campsite. It's late, 19.30, and Poppy hasn't yet been fed. She had a bag of crisps in the pub in Laleham, because what happened was that I walked into Staines, a very pretty walk, some lovely properties. It was too late to walk back. We got a bus and went into the Turks Head which is a nice pub. I had a couple of pints of Courage Best and a bag of nuts. Poppy had a bag of crisps. I'm going to feed her and myself and then that's going to be it for the night.

The Turks Head

Friendly and comfortable locals' pub with exposed timbers and brickwork. The function room area doubles as a small restaurant at lunchtimes.

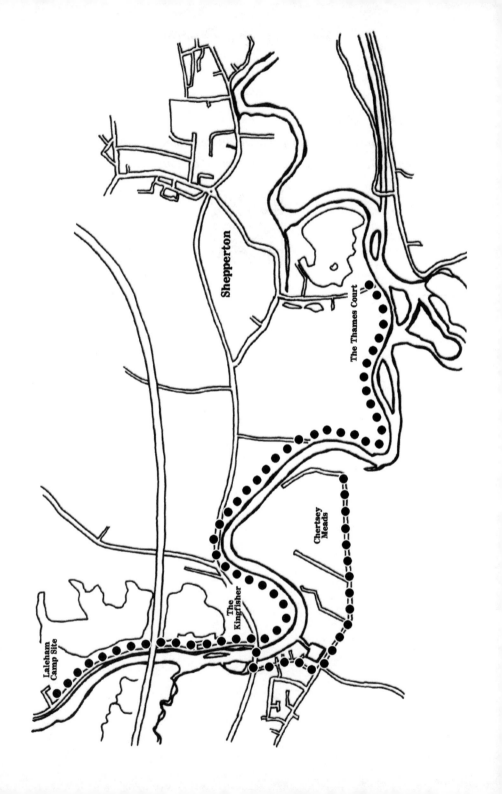

7.
Laleham via Chertsey to Shepperton (return)
14 April 2002

Well, it's Sunday morning and I've woken up to a beautiful April morning. Poppy and I have had our breakfast. Having a cup of coffee, then we will be off. It's 1030! Doesn't time go on?

I've taken a picture of a lovely little lock at Chertsey. And of the lovely bridge here. A little white stone, attractive bridge. There's a nice-looking pub here called The Kingfisher. It's a bit early but I will be back for a pint this evening. That will be my target today. To get back there just for one before my evening meal.

Believe it or not, I've just been treated to the sight of a woodpecker scooting along the Thames into a reed bed. What a beautiful sight. The blue on the kingfisher is quite uniquely beautiful.

I'm now walking across Chertsey Meads to Shepperton. A huge expanse of grass. It's hard to believe that we are so close to London.

Chertsey Lock

There was a pub there, called the Thames Court. Now that's a place that I don't understand. There was a queue for food the whole time that I was there. There was a huge amount of seating accommodation but these people, whole families, kids and all, were standing there queuing. Why would you do that? Why not get a seat and send one to the queue? Why bother anyway? There are loads and loads of other places along the Thames? Why not organise it so that someone got the punters comfortable and started selling them drinks?

I abandoned food. I'm not queuing for food. I haven't got where I am today by standing in a food queue whilst the bar is open. I found the bar. There were four or five people waiting to serve drinks at the bar. Nobody was buying because they were all queuing for food. Why organise a place like this? Put four or five people at the bar with nothing to do and one or two working their pants off at a never-ending queue for food.

The Thames Court, Shepperton

Overlooking the Thames our rather grand pub is a former ambassador's residence. With its Delph tiling, oak panelling and fireplaces it's an essential refreshment stop for ramblers and boaters. Fantastic gardens facing the Thames.

Poppy gave up here. She just didn't want to go on. She was happy to retrace our steps.

I had a pint at The Kingfisher but found that dogs weren't welcome. It was another food place!

The Kingfisher, Chertsey

The Kingfisher

Charming country pub/restaurant beside an 18th-century bridge, serving pub food classics and grills. Lovely riverside terrace.

We walked back to the campsite. And so now I am back at the van. Poppy has had her meal and she has gone to sleep. She's exhausted. She must be getting old. Whisper it, I'm not!

Oh, and for the record £2.35 per pint at The Kingfisher. I don't know. You have to be very wealthy like me to drink these days!

Ramblings of a Rambler

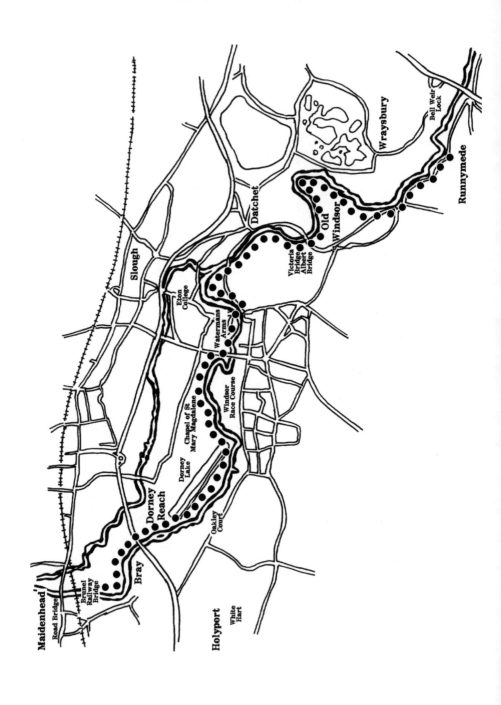

8.
Maidenhead to Runnymede
& the Bell Weir Lock
Saturday 29 March 2003.

Here I am again beginning another section of the Thames Walk. This time, I got the bus from home to Maidenhead and I've walked down to the riverside, where I am now.

I've made good time. It's only 0950. I've just taken a picture of Maidenhead road bridge. It's a beautiful, warm, sunny morning. In fact we have, believe it or not, enjoyed a period of twelve days of wonderful, warm spring weather, with no rain and sun every day.

Brunel's Maidenhead Bridge

On a personal diary note, Kiwi Dave from NZ and the rugby club and his wife Tessa have been with me now for two weeks and I'm enjoying their company. Tessa, who is a wonderful cook, is doing most of the cooking. I'm enjoying their company a lot more than Saddam Hussein is enjoying the company of the English and Americans and Spanish. That war is into its 12th day and it's hard to know how it's going.

I've just taken a couple of pictures of Brunel's railway bridge. The bridge that they said he couldn't build (bet that was a French man who said that). Defeatist buggers they are. It is known as the "Sounding Arch" because of the perfect echo that you can try out from the footpath underneath.

Brunel's "Sounding Arch"

This is interesting. There is a footbridge across the Thames here called the "Summerleaze" bridge that isn't in the Thames Walk book. It's just before Dorney Reach and there is a conveyor belt running merrily away from the north bank to the south. I haven't a clue what it's supposed to carry. It must be a mile long. It's a metaphor on life. It's not clear where it comes from. It isn't clear where it's going. And its purpose is unclear. But it looks like it could be quite an exciting ride.

"Oakley Court", home of the Hammer Horror Movies

On the south bank. A splendidly castellated structure, perhaps Tudor or even earlier. I must make it my business to find out. It has beautiful gardens along quite a long reach of the river. I've now turned over the page in my book and I find that it is Victorian Gothic and is called Oakley Court, built in 1859. Gosh, those Victorians knew a thing or two about looking after themselves.

And there's another lesson in life: "Don't say that you don't know something until you've turned over the next page." *

Turns out that Oakley Court is most famous for being the set for most of the Hammer horror films & other films, such as "The Brides of Dracula".

Dorney Lake

I've just taken a photo of Dorney Lake. I gather that it is a man-made lake, recently constructed for Eton College. It is quite unbelievable and must have cost millions of pounds.

I've also photographed two white vans which I think could possibly hold the Oxford Boat crew who are down here practising for the Boat Race. None of this is on the map book that I've got. Must be too recent. I'm now looking at the Chapel of St Mary Magdalene, at Boveney. It's a lovely, little old church of stone and brick with a wooden belfry that looks rather crooked. I imagine that it's looked crooked for years.

Chapel of Saint Mary Magdalene, Boveney

This church also featured in the Hammer horror films quite often.

Boveney Lock is, as a matter of interest, right by Windsor Racecourse. It is quarter past twelve and I'm sitting on a bench at a place called "Athens". The sun is a little hazy now but it's a beautiful day. I'm sitting looking across the river to Windsor Racecourse where the posh boys from Eton apparently bathe in the river. All is well with the world – especially if your dad's rich and you are at Eton College.

"Athens," Eton College's swimming spot

I've just had two pints of Courage Best at The Waterman's Arms, £2.05 per pint, built circa 1682. This is just off Eton High St. Quite a bargain. Also for future reference the food in there looked very nice and wasn't at all expensive.

Watermans, Eton

Built circa 1682, the deceptively large building has had a multitude of uses. It was originally the home of brewer Robert Style, and was formerly the Eton parish workhouse, before becoming a watering hole for the Watermen and Lightermen.

The original Watermans pub was next to a sawmill in Kings Stable Street; back then the street also housed Royal carriages and horses for Windsor Castle.

The riverbank and towpath is crammed with daffodils and is lovely. The bridge I'm photographing now is called Victoria Bridge. It's interesting because it's the place where you are forced off the south bank of the river because of security at Windsor Castle. I can see Windsor Castle in front of me. It's quite annoying that everywhere else along the bank people are doing their best to improve access to the river for the hoi polloi.

The one person doing bugger all about that is Her Majesty The Queen. How it can be that they can't arrange some sort of security fence that allows you to use the bank is beyond me.

John Holland was so incensed that he entered into correspondence with Her Majesty about it and got precisely nowhere. I don't think I will bother banging my head on that particular stone. I'm 60 shortly. Is this decision a sign of maturity?

I damn well hope not!

What happened here was that Queen Victoria demolished a bridge that went across the river to Datchet and built two new bridges. Victoria Bridge and Albert Bridge.

She did it to keep the public away from a stretch of the riverbank, so that she created her own riverside park. That's why to this date we mortals can't walk down the stretch between the two bridges.

You can bet what you like that the taxpayer at the time paid for both the bloody bridges.

And so here I am on Runnymede Meadows, probably the most famous meadow in the whole wide world because some years ago, Simon caught his first river eel here (and a major panic that caused when he had it on the end of his line).

Oh (and, by the way), it is also where the Magna Carta was signed in 1215 by King John. I suppose that was of some significance, too. Funnily enough, it was signed on Simon's birthday, 15 June!

I've just taken a photo from East Weir (Bell Weir) lock of the M25.

I've seen something remarkable. A guy has just caught a fish. During this walk I've passed hundreds of fisherman and I've seen hundreds pull in their lines whilst I was there, but I've never seen anyone catch anything. This guy caught a fish and it was all of four inches long.

Now you would have thought, in view of the number of hours that had been put in, to no avail, that catching one would have been an occasion. Something to celebrate. But this guy unhooked it and nonchalantly threw it back in. As if it were something he did every minute of every day. I was moved to clap but it's just as well that I didn't.

On my way home now. It is 1645 on Friday afternoon. The M25 is stationary. The biggest car park in the world. I popped into the White Hart for a pint. Nice beer, "Fuller's Summer Ale" £2.30 per pint. The food in there also looked good and was fairly priced. The rooms were a good price, too. Two people sharing £40 per night.

The White Hart

Tucked away in the sleepy Berkshire village of Holyport, the White Hart is a charming English pub oozing with character. The White Hart prides itself in being at the heart of the local community and focuses on offering delicious fresh food, great choice of real ale and a warm, friendly welcome to all.

It's a pub with two distinct halves: the lovely, dark wood-panelled lounge / dining bar displaying pictures of Holyport from years gone by, the perfect place for relaxed dining and drinking. The public bar: light and airy with wooden floors, bar billiards, television, occasional live music and gentle background music – something for everyone.

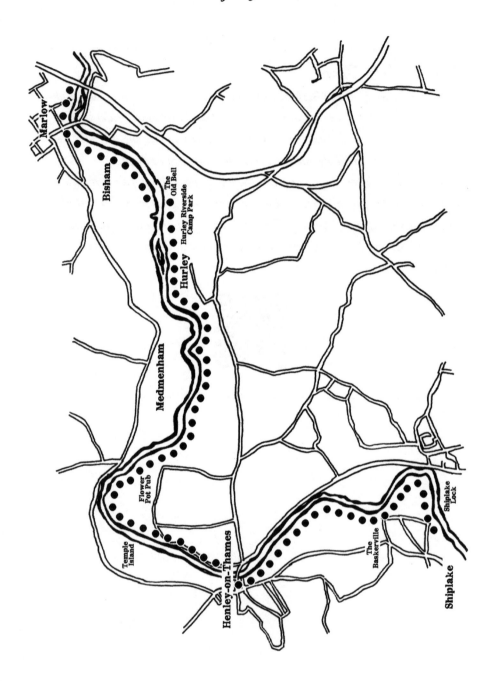

Marlow

Bisham

The Old Bell

Hurley Riverside Camp Park

Hurley

Medmenham

Flower Pot Pub

Temple Island

Henley-on-Thames

The Baskerville

Shiplake Lock

Shiplake

9.
Henley to Hurley, then to Shiplake

A much brighter day, although rain is forecast for later. I have begun again to walk the stretch from Henley to Marlow (*although from dad's notes it isn't obvious that he ever arrived at Marlow…).

Today the river is full of rowing teams and the towpath is cluttered with their cyclist coaches. I have taken some photos of Temple Island.

I also stopped to look at two tractors, Ferguson 35s, that must be 50 years old, but are still being used. They really took me back a few years!

Dad's old Tractors, the Ferguson 35!

I have also taken a photo of the Flower Pot Pub, which is a lovely short walk from Hambleden Lock, in the village of Aston. It's well worth a visit as it is a fascinating old pub that is completely unchanged inside. I doubt that it has been changed since it was built; coal fires, wooden floors – a dog asleep in a basket, tongue & groove painted walls, a soot-stained ceiling. Perfect time for a pint!

Flower Pot Pub, near Hambleden Lock

This pub is popular with walkers and angling enthusiasts. It is only a short walk from the Thames Path just outside Henley and it has the biggest display of stuffed freshwater fish in the UK, if not the world.

While you are admiring the collection of fish after their visit to the taxidermist, you'll find a number of other cartoons and pictures on the hunting and fishing theme. You can also enjoy some well-kept Brakspear beer and some wholesome pub food. The portions are generous and well able to restore the hungry walker.

The walk to Hurley is absolutely beautiful. It's a lovely day. At Hurley, the campsite attendant said it was £50 to camp, but he would do it for me for £10. I pointed out that there were no other campers. What a chancer…

I couldn't walk past the Olde Bell at Hurley without having a pint. After all, it had featured on one of a set of pub place mats that our family had used for the last 20 years.

I had John Smith's Smooth, only £1.45 a pint.

In 2019, The Olde Bell turned the grand old age of 884!

The Olde Bell first opened its doors in AD 1135 as a guest house for visitors to the nearby Benedictine Priory. For hundreds of years, the ringing of the Sanctus Bell signalled to the monks that an important visitor had arrived in the village and was on his way to call at their monastic retreat beside the River Thames. The Sanctus Bell still hangs over the door of The Olde Bell, a sign of welcome and refreshment to travellers.

There is a secret passage running from the cellar of The Olde Bell to the Priory in the village. The secret passage was used by Lord Lovelace of Hurley who was a plotter of the 'Glorious Revolution' in 1688 which drove the Catholic James II into exile and placed his son-in-law William of Orange jointly with his wife, James's daughter Mary, on the throne.

The Olde Bell was an important staging point on the Oxford to London route, with the last recorded schedule in 1890.

In 1936 the 17th-century malthouse was the residence of the classic horror actor Boris Karloff whilst he was making "Juggernaut" & "The Man Who Changed His Mind". His wife Dorothy said of Hurley: "It's the loveliest, tiniest village you can imagine."

During World War Two, famous guests at The Olde Bell included Sir Winston Churchill, Dwight D. Eisenhower and Colonel Elliott Roosevelt, son of the wartime President, who were all visiting Ladye Place mansion, next to the church, which was being used as a secret US intelligence base prior to the Normandy landings. Also, during wartime, the two barns were turned into a small arms factory, producing bullets, with a labour force of Hurley ladies.

Some notable guests have included Elizabeth Taylor, Richard Burton, Cary Grant and Errol Flynn. We have more recently played host to some location filming for Dustin Hoffman on his directorial debut and are also a bit of a favourite secret escape for some very recognisable faces.

The Olde Bell has had many owners during its long history, but despite its many changes of ownership, it still keeps to the traditions of Saint Benedict – that true hospitality be provided to travellers and strangers.

Arranged over five buildings, guests will be treated to a wide range of choice when it comes to accommodation.

Map 8 (continued)

The next morning I caught a bus from the campsite at Hurley back to Henley. I then walked south down the river to Shiplake.

At Shiplake I took some photos of Shiplake Lock, then had a pint in The Baskerville Arms, Lower Shiplake, £2.20 for a pint of Brakspear.

Set in a red-brick building, this classic country pub with rooms sits adjacent to National Rail trains in the village of Lower Shiplake. It's a three-minute walk from the River Thames.

I also took some photos at Fairacres, a huge house that had a railway running through the garden!

Shiplake is named after a place either where sheep were washed in the river (sheep-lake) or where a Viking ship sank, back in the day (Ship-Loss). One is certainly more glamorous than the other.

What is certain, though, is that the year I was born (on 13 November 1943) an American Flying Fortress, B-17 bomber "Sunrise Serenader" crashed in the riverside fields at Shiplake with the tail falling in what is now Hennerton Golf Club. Nine crewmen died and one managed to parachute to safety. Two bombs exploded.

Maybe they found bits of the Viking ship in there whilst they were fishing it out!

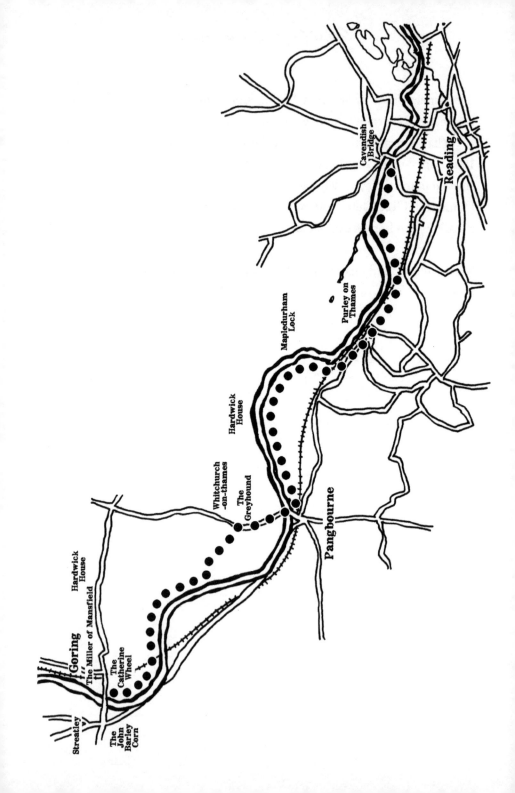

10.
Caversham to Goring
23 April 2004

It is St George's Day and here I am at Caversham Bridge in Reading, beginning another section of the Thames Walk.

It is only 0930 and I've got here by bus to Bourne End, train to Maidenhead and train to Reading.

Believe it or not, Thames Trains played the platform race game on me at Maidenhead and I lost again. It isn't a difficult game. Your connecting train is sitting at the departure platform when you pull in, slightly late.

The idea is that you have to fight the crowds to get off your train. Fight your way along the platform to the subway steps. Fight your way through the throng of humanity, all coming up the stairs that you wish to descend. Fight your way through the crowd coming through the subway and down the steps from the train that you are now racing to catch. Then, if you are lucky, you get to the train before the staff wave it away.

I got to the train just as the doors closed and it pulled away without me! I didn't lynch anyone and in truth only had about fifteen minutes to wait for the next train…

…Oh, and I am retired! It used to get me so wound up when I worked.

There was a young man on the platform and he latched onto me throughout our wait and travelled all the way to Reading with me. He was indeed a very knowledgeable young man putting the world to rights – his rights. He was very critical of George Bush and Tony Blair and their joint adventures in Iraq. It was indeed an interesting discussion.

I popped into "The Carnival Stores". I bought the gliders and parachutes for the annual rugby club trip to Arnhem next week (a compulsory prop). I also got two St George's Day flags which are now proudly decorating my knapsack.*
The Carnival Stores sadly closed, after 77 years, in 2011.

Diary note. It's a wonderful morning. Not a cloud in the sky. This is unusual this year. We have had some pretty awful weather. Wet and cold and miserable. This is the best day so far, but then I always plan my walks on good days, don't I?

I'm at Tilehurst. It's 1100. I've taken my time, wandering along a lovely stretch of the river.

Some beautiful properties. I've used my new camera to the full. Because I can just dump any picture (image in modern parlance) that I don't want to keep. I have to leave the river here because, apparently, the footbridge further upstream is being repaired. The path therefore is diverted (at considerable expense), up the bank, by way of a scaffolding arrangement, through Tilehurst station.

Lovely little boat here on the other bank, where someone seems to have their own little Thames-side plot. A boat, a shed, what more would you want?

Heaven.

I've just seen a black swan on the river. Unusual? Unusual for me anyway.

I am standing on the riverbank at Pangbourne, looking along the sweep of the Thames to Mapledurham Lock with Hardwick House on the opposite bank. There is a beautiful Tudor mansion house, where Elizabeth I stayed and apparently Charles I played lawn bowls here whilst he was imprisoned nearby, after the English Civil War.

I stopped to admire a beautiful, delicate little sedge bunting singing away in a patch of reeds. A lovely bird with a lovely song.

I stopped for lunch in "The Greyhound" in Whitchurch village. What a cracking pub! In there was a party of guys setting off on a St George's Day piss-up. I took a picture of them and they took a picture of me. I observed them from afar with some admiration. The torture that they will put themselves through today, the self-sacrifice to St George and Old England, their complete unselfish abandonment to the cause. These things go on all the time and very little acknowledgement ever accrues.

The Greyhound, Whitchurch-on-Thames

The pub is a former ferryman's cottage in the picturesque village of Whitchurch-on-Thames, featuring low beams, a log fire and a small, sheltered back garden. Ideally situated for those making the most of the Thames Path, or cruising the river, we can offer the weary traveller a tasty and filling meal or light bite and a refreshing ale or soft drink to help them on their way.

We are also close to the mainline railway and there are bus stops in the village serving Reading and the surrounding area. Children, dogs and their well-behaved guardians are welcome (although we would ask that dogs please keep their owners on a lead).

St George's Day celebrations!

Now I am back on the track. It's 1415 I will see how far I can get for the rest of the day. I hope to reach Goring. Now I see the first lilac out. It looks absolutely gorgeous.

Unbelievable. Here I am on the banks of the Thames between Whitchurch and Goring and here on the bank is a concrete pillbox, left over from our internal defences during the war.

The question is: who the hell thought that the Germans might invade Oxford via the bloody River Thames? And why would they? What were they afraid of? Exploding Latin books?

Second World War concrete pillboxes

I'm rethinking this. I don't think that the bloody boxes are to watch for Germans coming up the river in rubber dinghies. I think it could be something to do with the fact that the main east-west railway line goes over the bridge. Maybe that was what these things were put here for.

What the then Ministry of Defence didn't know was that the British Rail people at Maidenhead would make it impossible for anyone to get past them anyway!

For God's sake, it's difficult enough in peacetime. Why was all this war effort spent on defending this line when all they had to do was tell the British Rail staff at Maidenhead to be just a trifle more difficult with the Germans than they would be on a normal weekday, with their English customers. No one would have got past them. Actually, I'm now beginning to wonder if the tactics at Maidenhead are a leftover from the war?

Maybe no one has told them that the war is over, that they need no longer make it so bloody difficult for people to catch their trains. That everyone is not a Nazi. Maybe someone should tell them. But then again, wouldn't it just wreck their day if they couldn't screw someone up?

A little further on there is a wild flower garden. Three guys appeared to be installing a nesting box in a tree. A huge box! I've no idea what it might be for.

I waved to one of the chaps who was sitting on the ground. The bastard just ignored me. How rude is that? Out in the countryside, with no one about, someone waves and you bloody well ignore them. He had a mauve shirt on. Bets are that he's a pinky, left-wing liberal git, who objected to me invading his space. Oh he's coming along now on his bike. I think I will shove a stick in his wheel as he passes. Bring him off into this mud!

I've walked through this wild flower garden, apparently preserved by the good people of Goring. In this garden are: cuckoo flower, cowslips, and believe it or not, several snake's head fritillaries, that's a beautiful wild flower. People will say how the hell did John know that: well, how much do I know?

I have arrived at Goring and Streatley station, to catch a train that left Oxford at 1701 and was due here at 1731. A half-hour journey. It's now 1752 and they are expecting it to arrive in two minutes. It's lost half an hour on its journey from Oxford, which is a half-hour journey. It's unbelievable! These people couldn't run a piss-up in a brewery.

Maybe, on the other hand, that's the only thing they could actually organise. They are completely, completely useless.

I am at Reading railway station now. This is interesting. It's now 1825 and believe it or not, no one has any idea what time there will be a train to Maidenhead. A British Rail employee has just told me to stay put on platform 10, not to go to platform 6, which has been closed down for some reason.

This advice was given by a chap in the uniform of Great Western. I wonder what they are good at? It isn't running railways.

One of dad's mates from
British Rail......

1830. A young lady has just asked the Great Western man if he would open the ladies' toilet on this platform. He replied that it would be opened at 1915, not before, because it gets vandalised on this little-used platform, which is thronged with people.

In the meantime the toilets were open on platform 6. She said, quite understandably, that she had been told to wait here for a train and that if she went she may miss it. In any case she said platform 6 was closed! Isn't life wonderful!?

A train came into platform 9 which was announced as a through train to Paddington. I asked the driver if he would slow down as he went through Maidenhead so that I could leap off. He said he couldn't, because the doors locked until the train was stationary. However, he found me on the platform and told me to get on the train because he had been told to terminate the train at Slough. He reckoned that I would get back to Maidenhead quicker from Slough. So I did.

I'm in 1st Class of this very full train. I will move if I have to, but I can't imagine anyone risking his neck to check tickets tonight. The word is going around that all these good people who thought that they were on an express to Paddington are to be dumped at Slough. There could be a lynching.

Aren't I glad to be out of all this? This was a daily experience for me and is a daily experience for all these poor bloody people.

By the way, that beer at the pub by the station at Goring was the worst pint I have had in a long time. £2.20 Greene King IPA. Awful. Warm. Imagine my chagrin when I was told that the train was half an hour late and I had to go back and drink a pint of Foster's lager.*

The John Barleycorn

The John Barleycorn is situated at Goring-on-Thames in stunning Oxfordshire countryside and within a short walk of the River Thames. A warm and friendly welcome is waiting for all that visit us.

The John Barleycorn's first recorded use as an 'alehouse' was in 1810. It is thought that the railway workers building the line through Goring were its first bunch of regulars. The building itself dates from the 17th century. Formerly three cottages knocked into one building, it has customary original oak beams, low ceilings and uneven floors! There are two bars, a public bar with a real fireplace for a warmer in the winter months, also a lounge bar with its own entrance and is situated next to the restaurant where customers can enjoy a pre-dinner drink if they so choose.

*Dad's notes do not say which pub this awful beer was experienced in, but most likely the Catherine Wheel, or possibly, just because he would have… The John Barleycorn… which is also in Goring.

1855 I am now at Slough station and I have been informed by a Great Western man that the next train will depart from the platform that I am on but he's not that sure when. "Stay put," he said. All the people on the train that I just came in on who thought they were on an express to Paddington are traipsing down the platform to board a stopping train to Paddington. Still no one has been lynched. "Come, friendly bombs and fall on Slough".

Home at last 2105. Unbelievable.

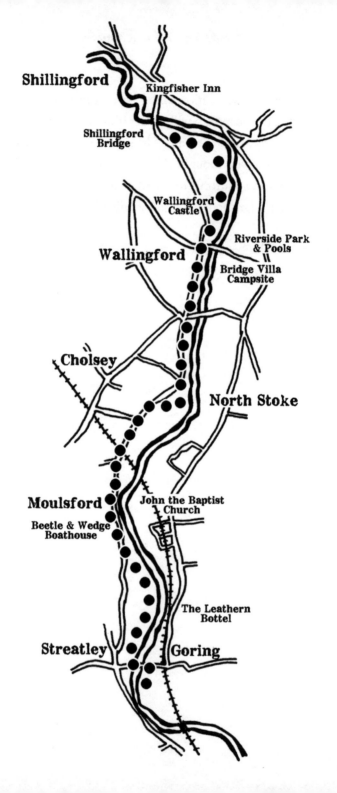

Shillingford

Kingfisher Inn

Shillingford
Bridge

Wallingford
Castle

Riverside Park
& Pools

Wallingford

Bridge Villa
Campsite

Cholsey

North Stoke

Moulsford

John the Baptist
Church

Beetle & Wedge
Boathouse

The Leathern
Bottel

Streatley

Goring

11.
Goring to Shillingford & The "Red Wine Rush" Saturday 15 May 2004

I'm 61 tomorrow and I'm picking up the walk at Goring Lock.

Goring Lock

1015 am, it's a beautiful day. I'm in shorts and a T-shirt. Yesterday I travelled to Wallingford and camped at the little campsite by the river.

This morning I got a bus to Goring station about which I wrote with some feeling last time I was in this area.

Goring and Streatley are wonderful little Thames-side villages. This is where the Ridgeway footpath meets the Thames.

What is surprising here is just how wide the river is. I'm looking at a system of weirs, just upstream from Goring. The river must be 400 yards wide here. If I remember rightly, when I was in Staines, the river was only 20 or 30 yards wide. Which is a puzzle, isn't it?

Where does all the water go? Is it extracted? Does it leak out? Do the cows drink it?

The Leatherne Bottel

Was a nice pub/restaurant, now an upscale Italian restaurant. How sad. I am sure that they will still sell you an (overpriced) Italian lager, though...

How lovely. There's a little sailing boat, obviously from the next door sailing club. England's Green and Pleasant Land!

I'm in Ferry Lane at Moulsford. There's another Brunel bridge here!

Had a bit of luck just now. I was talking to a lady and gentleman mooring their boat outside the pub here, "The Beetle & Wedge". She advised me that a new stretch of the path has been opened.

The Beetle & Wedge

The Beetle & Wedge Boathouse is a restaurant set on the site of the original Moulsford ferry service, on the banks of the River Thames on Ferry Lane in Moulsford, Oxfordshire, England. The restaurant has a riverside setting on the very same stretch of river immortalised in The Wind in the Willows, and also Jerome K. Jerome's chronicles of the escapades of his friends in Three Men in a Boat. The unusual name refers to a beetle, an old term for a maul (or hammer) used with a wedge to split wood.

In 2005 the restaurant played host to Griff Rhys Jones, Dara Ó Briain and Rory McGrath, and a dog called Loli, during the filming of Three Men in a Boat – a film broadcast and commissioned by the BBC as a modern-day reinterpretation of the travelogue by Jerome K. Jerome.

The building that houses the restaurant was once a working boathouse and was last used for the ferry in 1967, when the last ferrywoman retired and the service was discontinued. The boathouse retains much of its original fittings and sits on the water's edge with the original slipway still in place. The building actually dates back to before 1860 when it was a trading inn.

I thought that I would have to walk for a couple of miles along the road but she said, "No, there's a new bridge just along the road." It's apparently near a boys' college. This is a relief because my plan was to cross on the ferry to the Ridgeway path which follows the opposite bank. There isn't now a ferry. It stopped ages ago.

The Beetle & Wedge is a famous pub, made famous by H.G. Wells, George Bernard Shaw and Jerome K. Jerome.

Now I am on the road and I can see a sign "Thames Path – Wallingford 4 miles". So it is 4 miles back to the campsite. It's only 1105 so I will be there by lunchtime.

I had a nice sandwich and a couple of pints of Greene King Ale in a pub in Wallingford. £2.40 per pint – very nice.

1430 and I'm off again. I think I just saw a yellowhammer (yellow bird, long tail, very yellow under its breast, black on its tail), flying over the river. Dipping up and down. Not dipping into the river. Could it be a wagtail?

And because it's May, the swifts and the swallows are back from Africa. What's that – 10,000 miles? They always get back during the first two weeks in May.

The blue and white flower that I have seen so much of could be loosehead strife.

Here I am at Shillingford and I've taken a photo of the bridge.

Shillingford Bridge

It's 1620 and perhaps time that I started looking for a bus back. So I got to Shillingford and found the pub was closed!

The Kingfisher

The Kingfisher is no longer a pub, but a family-operated hotel (with five rooms).

But I found a bus stop and was there only five minutes before a bus came along. On the way back to Wallingford, we stopped at Benson and the driver got out, locked the doors and told me he was going for a cup of tea! Back at the campsite in Wallingford now. Had my dinner. Not going anywhere tonight. Had a couple of pints in town and intend to turn in early. My impressions of Wallingford are not good. I had been looking forward to coming. Somehow, I had it in my mind that it would be a lovely Thames-side town, but it isn't really. It's missing a wonderful opportunity. It's noisy and trashy.

I'm now watching the couple in the next van. They are eating outside and donning more and more clothes as the evening progresses. The guy has been drinking loads of red wine and now has what I call "The Red Wine Rush". It's sort of the opposite of a high. He has a cream cracker in his lips but doesn't seem to know what to do with it.

When the meal began he was expansive. His arm and hand gestures were elaborate. He talked all the way through the meal, impressing the young lady who has come with his interesting and probably entertaining conversation. But he has polished off a full bottle of red wine and he is now in "The Red Wine Rush."

He is showing the classic symptoms. His pupils keep disappearing into the tops of his eye sockets. His head has sunk slowly but surely and is now resting on his chest. Oh – he's found another bottle. He's filled his glass again. This man is a drinking legend. Just think he probably spends his days doing things far less important, like work.

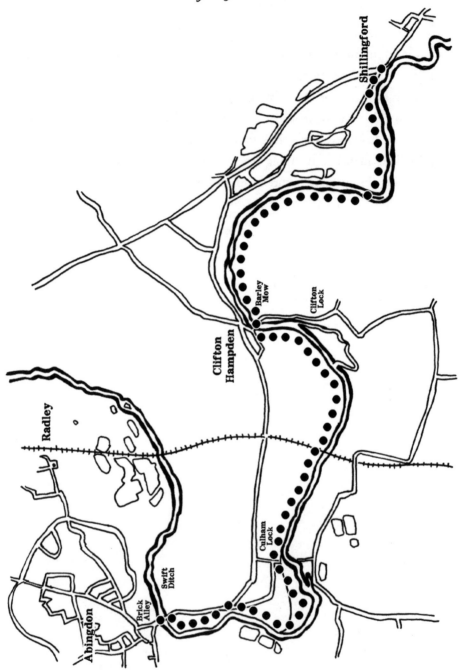

12.
Abingdon to Shillingford
4 June 2004

Well, here I am again, coming up to the 60th anniversary of D-Day.

I was one year old and remember it well! There are lots of celebrations planned in France and Italy.

What's happening in England right now? Tony Blair is still PM. He's struggling because of the Iraq War. It hasn't gone to plan at all. Many of the "liberated" Iraqis are turning on the soldiers who liberated them. It's all looking a mess, but then things often look a mess before they begin to look better. And you can't make an omelette without breaking an egg or two.

I've just had my 61st birthday and we are just coming up to Simon's 32nd birthday next week.

Phillip, Tania and Anna are still in Australia.

Here I am. I have just camped at a little place called Clifton Hampden Camp Site. An absolutely gorgeous little campsite on the banks of the Thames. My plan tomorrow is to walk from here, downriver hopefully, to where I left off at Shillingford. It's a lovely evening. I've put my new windbreak up.

Believe it or not, there is a thatched pub, on the corner of the site called the Barley Mow. It claims to be 650 years old and one that Jerome K.

Jerome, author of one of my favourite books, *Three Men in a Boat*, used to frequent. I have absolutely no doubt that I shall sample their wares before the evening is out.

The campsite is a bloody disgrace. There is no hot water. The toilets are filthy. The washbasins are filthy. There's a fat witch that looks after it. She was so idle that she dealt with me entirely through the kitchen window – shouting all the time.

She didn't actually say that I was a bloody nuisance, but I knew that was what she meant. Not somewhere that you would bring the family to.

Clifton Hampden campsite taken from the riverbank

It's 1030 next day and I have changed my mind. I have decided to walk from Abingdon to Shillingford. I got a bus to Abingdon.

Diary note – you can hire day boats here for river trips. You can also moor free for five days on the banks of the river.

Here on the banks of the river are some beautiful old almshouses in Brick Alley, Abingdon. They apparently date from 1446.

Beautiful almshouses dating from 1446 in Brick Alley, Abingdon

I have reached Swift Ditch, which was once the main River Thames until the monks at Abingdon built their lock and caused the Thames to divert. The landscape around here has probably not changed much over hundreds of years.

And now, not ten paces on, modernity. Didcot Power Station forms our backdrop – in all its glory.

Two water birds. One charcoal-grey body with black neck. White blaze on face. The other white face, white stripe down its breast, some brown on its head and sporting what looks distinctly like ears.

Culham Lock

*The next time Dad was here we were on the 2013 boat trip. Our boat ran aground and broke down twice (and Dad drove it into Clifton Hampden Bridge the following day) but the first breakdown occurred whilst trying to negotiate this lock.

There's a sign here – it says that Clifton Hampden is three miles. It's 1130. I will probably have my lunch at the Barley Mow. I will use their toilets!

This is where the Culham Cut rejoins the Thames proper. Culham Cut was created in 1809 to bypass a twisting stretch of the river.

There's a field here. It's a field of wheat. It is right on the bank of the Thames. It must be half a mile wide and it stretches from Didcot Power Station and ends at the weir where the Clifton Cut begins.

I've met some people here. A couple. They started at Culham today and they intend to walk today to Oxford. It's 1230. That's a walk of thirteen miles before the end of the day. What's the pleasure in that?

This is one huge field. No doubt very efficient to farm but think, will you, of the vandalism that the farmer (a steward of the countryside) has done to the landscape. Think how many hedges and habitats he has wrecked in pursuit of his own selfish business ambitions.

Walkers – think about all the various beauty you have experienced along the Thames Path and know what beauty this selfish bastard has wrecked. He should be shot at dawn. Think then, if you will, that he was encouraged in his vandalism by the tenants of the EU's Common Agricultural Policy, which paid him money, out of taxes, and so compelled him to produce more and more corn which Europe could not consume and the taxpayer had to fork out again to dispose of the surplus.

What an abomination!

All along this stretch, this morning, the trees are decorated with dog roses. Mostly pink, but some are white. All seem to have put themselves there for the sheer enjoyment of the passer-by.

Clifton Lock

There's a heron standing in the field just in front of me. I thought I could quietly get close but a couple of bicycle riders came along. They stopped with me to see but then moved off and the heron took fright.

Now I see the campsite on the opposite bank and I can see Clifton Hampden Bridge with Clifton Hampden church in the background.

Diary note: £3 to moor your boat on the bank opposite the campsite.

It's 1 o'clock. I propose to go over the bridge* and enjoy a pint and a sandwich at the Barley Mow.

Clifton Hampden Bridge, which dad crashed our boat into in 2013

Jerome K. Jerome described Clifton Hampden as "a wonderfully pretty village, old-fashioned, peaceful and dainty with flowers".

All is well in this wonderful world!

The Barley Mow

The Barley Mow is a thatched country tavern in the little village of Clifton Hampden. More than 650 years old, the pub is packed with original features and visitors have admired and enjoyed this country inn for centuries, including renowned writers like Jerome K. Jerome and Charles Dickens Jnr. Stepping inside this glorious thatched tavern is like taking a step back in time. The Barley Mow pub shows off a host of original features including low beams and an old fireplace so large it fits across two different parts of the pub. Our superb menu offers traditional pub food and seasonal dishes that cater for the whole family. The Barley Mow is a storybook pub nestled in the picturesque little village and civil parish of Clifton Hampden, just over three miles east of Abingdon, Oxfordshire. Famous English writer, Jerome K. Jerome, depicted this part of the River Thames area beautifully in his classic 1889 book Three Men in a Boat as "the wonderfully pretty village, old-fashioned, peaceful and dainty with flowers". In Anglo-Saxon times Clifton Hampden was known as 'tun on a cliff' (town on a cliff), a name allegedly given because of the rock face that stands above the rest of the village. Perched on the top of this cliff, just five minutes from the Barley Mow pub, is the historic church of St Michael & All Angels, a chapel of the Dorchester parish until the 19th century.

There is a wide range of beers in here. I've chosen Theakstons which is the weakest and it's delicious – £2.40. So what I did was I had two pints of that lovely beer and then realised that I was within a few yards of my camper van, where I had chicken and pork and lettuce and tomatoes etc etc.

So I returned there where I had a light feast of chicken salad. The chicken cost £3.40 last week. I had a meal out of it at home. I had a meal last night. A lunch today and I have put some in my little deep freezer. People whinge about not having enough money to eat. I don't understand.

I am off again now. Heading towards Shillingford. There's a crossbill here in the river. It's now holding its wings out to dry. Its wings are more than six feet across.

And so I arrived at Shillingford and bused back to Clifton Hampden.

*This would be the very same Clifton Hampden Bridge that Dad drove into during our annual boat trip on 12 May 2013.

"can't think how that happened….."

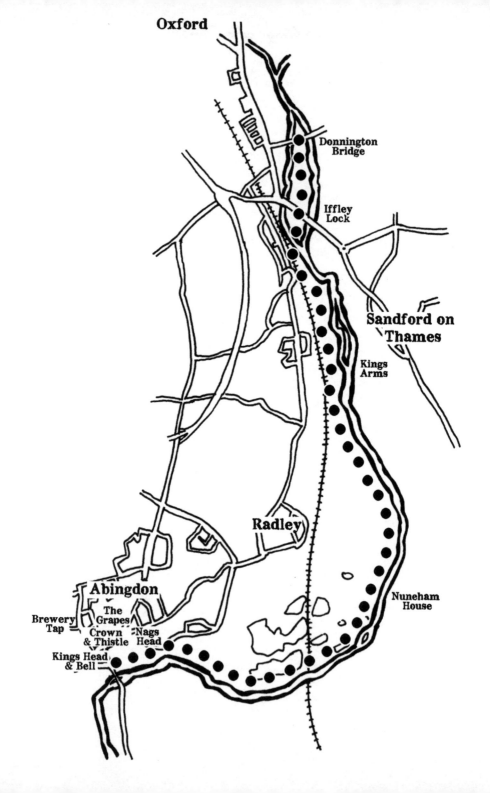

13.
Iffley Lock, Sandford
& Abingdon
7 June 2007

I've walked to Sandford Lock, dictating my stories all along the way, and I now realise that my recorder hasn't been working. I am sitting on a bench to see if I can catch up.

There's a guy jogging past me. He has a water bottle tucked down the back of his shorts. He looks about 136 and looks completely knackered. He probably thinks that it's all a good idea. I'm not so bloody sure. There is a queue for the lock. The lock gates have just opened and the boats are chugging past me into the lock.

All is well with my immediate little world. I will now try to relate the day's walk so far…

I left the Oxford Camping & Caravanning Club campsite, an adequate site, near the Park and Ride facility at Oxford.

I walked to Donnington Bridge where I joined the Thames Path. I've had a very pleasant walk downstream on the south bank through beautiful water meadows. They contain only cows and wild flowers. The idea is that these meadows flood when there is too much water and hold the surge so that places downstream don't get inundated.

The water is then released through the weir systems, at a pace that will not cause floods. That's the theory.

I've taken lots of pictures of Iffley Lock and its approaches.

Iffley Lock

My book extolled the virtues of the church at Iffley. I saw the Norman tower, so crossed the river and paid a visit. I took many pictures. It was an absolutely delightful church. Well worth the detour.

A lovely, leisurely walk to Sandford where I stopped for a couple of pints of Courage Discovery Summer Ale at The Kings Arms. I walked a little further, found a bench and enjoyed my packed lunch. Lewis Carroll was a vicar, you know, and he used to preach in the Norman church here.

The Kings Arms, Sandford

The Kings Arms is situated by the riverside in Sandford-on-Thames, Oxford, and is a traditional pub restaurant with al fresco dining in those hot summer days. Retaining traditional features including three old open fireplaces, although only one is in working order. The particular feature of this lovely pub is the garden which overlooks the river with stunning views and barbeques in the summer. The children love it here as they can see the ducks and swans while parents relax in a peaceful and tranquil setting. The food at The Kings Arms is rooted in traditional British cuisine and the chefs showcase a modern flair with the dishes they produce.

A Salter's Steamer is passing by. It looks capable of holding 400 people. There are about two dozen old-age pensioners on-board. I see that the back deck is loaded with life-savers. Floats that would be thrown in for those on the sinking ship to swim to.

I can't believe they would be any bloody use for the bunch of old codgers on-board today. Let's pray that it doesn't go down.

Part of my lunch today was a bag of Walkers crisps. They didn't taste that good. When I checked the "use by" date I found it to be October 2001. I gave them to the ducks. They can't read!

1515 I'm at Abingdon. That walk has taken five hours but I have wandered off the track and had many stops. An enjoyable walk.

Dad walking into Abingdon at the start of our sesh in 2013!

I'm now back at the campsite. I caught a bus into Abingdon. I wandered around Abingdon, as you do, went into a pub, The Kings Head & Bell. The landlord came over and asked what I would like. I was about to order a beer when the music clicked in at 5,000 decibels. I said, "It's too noisy for me."

The Kings Head & Bell

The Kings Head & Bell Abingdon is a 16th-century coaching inn set deep in the heart of the beautiful market town of Abingdon-on-Thames, with stylish, modern touches alongside the beautiful character of this 500-year-old building.

I went around the corner to another pub, The Crown & Thistle, and asked for a pint of bitter. They didn't sell beer, just lagers, Guinness, 1664 which the French call "Seize" and which I can drink in France because they don't sell decent beer and Seize is the least obnoxious of what is available there.

I asked if they could direct me to a real ale pub. They suggested the pub round the corner – the noisy one. They then suggested The Grapes around the corner. The Grapes doesn't sell real ale either just stouts, lagers and bloody Seize.

The Grapes
TripAdvisor Feb 2019

"A Proper Pub". An old-school pub with a good mix of locals young and old. Great for watching sport or a game darts or cribbage. The staff are very friendly and occasionally the landlord will pull a pint or two. Great as a local or a stopover on the way to an event like football or rugby matches. Cheap prices and good town centre location. Well worth a visit for a pint or ten and a bag of crisps if in Abingdon.

The landlord suggested the Broad Face, an excellent pub apparently, won lots of prizes for its beer. I went there, got a pint of Morland's.

The Broad Face

"The Broad Face sits in the heart of Abingdon. Its aim is to be a quality pub showcasing the best of local produce and welcoming to locals and visitors alike.

The Broad Face public house is at the junction of Bridge Street and Thames Street. The building was erected in 1840 but there are records of a public house called the Broad Face as far back as 1734. Mystery surrounds the origin of the Broad Face's name. Some say it's to do with its riverside location, as the building presents a broad face to the Thames.

Much more colourful are the theories that it alludes either to the swollen face of a man who drowned in the river, or the bloated face of a man who was hanged at the gaol that used to be opposite the pub".

It was awful, absolute piss. I had a pint of Seize and a pint of Foster's. From a beer point of view, a disappointing day. It's been very hot and you are up against it in a pub when it's hot, but I serve good beer in the rugby club whether it's hot or cold.

These people are just not trying. The young lady behind the bar at The Grapes helpfully advised me where to get the bus to Oxford. She also advised that the Broad Face had good ale.

Her advice about the bus was sound. Her advice about the Broad Face was hopelessly off course.

It's a real shame, for Abingdon, because the brewers Morland are based here and they came up with the beer Old Speckled Hen in Abingdon, apparently to celebrate one of the first MG cars that was built here, which had that nickname.

The next time Dad & I visited Abingdon was in 2013 when we had a super afternoon in The Nags Head on the bridge, so suggest you try that if you want to visit the town!

A better pub experience in Abingdon, in 2013, in the Nags Head on the bridge….left to right, Gary Sheppard, Mike Pendleton, me, Simon, dad and Hawkprat

The Nags Head

The Nags Head is situated halfway across Abingdon Bridge, positioned in the middle of the Thames with riverside gardens nestled in the stunning surroundings of Nag's Island.

A peaceful retreat amongst the rushes and willows providing many comfortable areas for families and diners to enjoy the best outdoor dining in Abingdon.

After a prolonged closure, the pub has been fitted out delightfully with the main bar at "bridge level" serving real ales, excellent wines, coffee, bar meals and à la carte menu.

The Nags Head has won the CAMRA Town and Country 'Pub of the Year' three times and has featured in The Good Beer Guide 2014, 2015, 2016, 2017 & 2018!

It's eight o'clock and I have had a pint at The Fox & Hounds.

The Fox and Hounds is local pub located just outside Newbury in Donnington, with a bar and restaurant. It is owned and run by the Vine family. The Vine's

have been serving Newbury for over 50 years, through Newbury's popular local butchers shop, Griffins, which is located on the bridge in Newbury high street. After purchasing the pub and refurbishing it, the Fox and Hounds free house has been transformed into a great local pub for fine ales and excellent quality food. Enjoy a refreshing drink with one of the fine ales or choose one of the mouth watering dishes on the menu, all made using fresh local produce, in a relaxed, friendly atmosphere.

There are several new arrivals on the site. The first thing they all bloody do is fix up their satellite disks. There is a guy opposite on the roof of his van, on a mobile phone getting advice on which way to point his dish.

Oh hell, the guy next to me and the one next to him are fixing their dishes. They're on a few days' camping and will spend their evenings watching *EastEnders* or *Coronation Street* or some other banal crap.

I think if I were still married and out here camping (which of course wouldn't have happened, by the way), my guess is that I would be fixing up a dish and looking forward to a fascinating night watching banality on a stupid box.

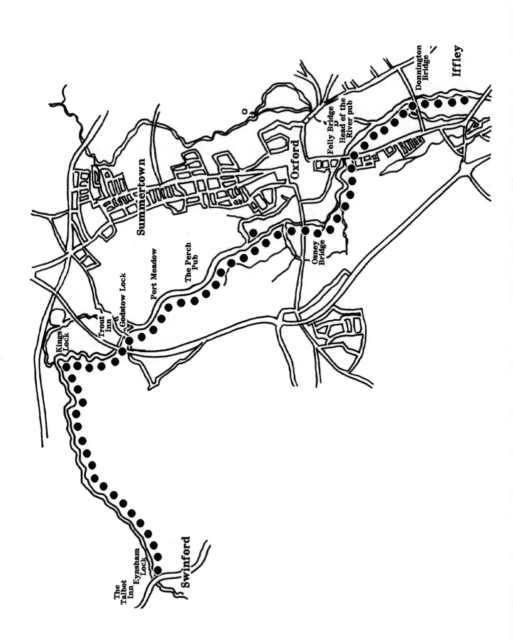

14.
Donnington to Swinford, via Oxford
8 & 9 June 2007

A lovely day. I walked from the site back to Donnington Bridge and this time turned upriver. There is a well-made and well-used path here to Oxford, about one mile. A pleasant walk to Folly Bridge and The Head of the River Pub.

I wandered around the town and found my way to Worcester College, where my eldest brother Tony studied for his degree. The college grounds are lovely. There is a large lake and it is a very peaceful setting. It still amazes me that in those 1950s days, the education system could "find" my brother, one of seven children who grew up in a small, rural Lancashire village.

Oxford itself was bloody awful. It was very, very hot and swarming with people. And now I can sadly report that, apart from one pub, I couldn't find a good pint of English ale either at Abingdon or at Oxford.

There have been hundreds of years of learning at this place. We have turned out world-beating scholars in all disciplines, but we haven't passed on the noble tradition of ale brewing.

Hundreds and thousands of tourists come here to see the gleaming spires and sample a taste of traditional England and in the pubs we serve them piss. Australian or Continental lagers that taste just as good as those at home abound. Imagine trying to get a taste of English ale in any of the homelands of these bloody tourists. It just wouldn't happen.

And yet in what should be one of the most English of English places, all you have in the pubs is a vast choice of imported piss...

The one exception was a pub called The Head of the River which I looked at and discarded because it was an absolute jungle of people. In desperation I went in there. I had two pints of Fuller's Discovery beer. It was well kept and it was refreshingly cool. That is the first time that has happened in the last two days.

Head of the River

This stunning and popular riverside pub, with fabulous bedrooms, huge terrace and all-day dining, offers a rollicking Oxford experience in the heart of the city.

The hotel flanks a delightful riverside terrace on two sides with historic Folly Bridge on the other. It is next to Christ Church Meadow, while Oxford's colleges, museums, galleries, shops and theatres are all within a ten-minute stroll. For more energetic guests, punts and river cruisers leave the opposite bank, while the Ice Rink and Hinksey Park Lido are close by.

The Head of the River pub, Oxford

I walked back to the site, passed The Fox & Hounds, but wasn't tempted, as I was last night, to pop in for a flyer. What a scruffy hole that place is! I am in my camper van now, reading my book, *How Mumbo-Jumbo Conquered the World*, which is a great read. I shall have another beer, then my meal, "steak au poivre", with a side salad and copious red wine.

Bless you, John.

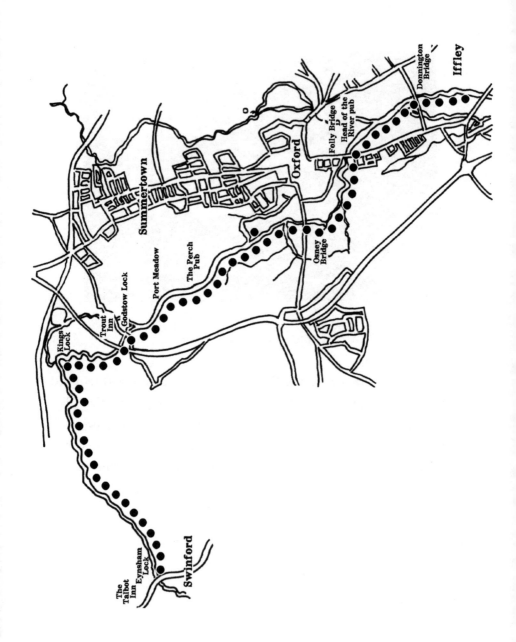

Donnington to Swinford
9 June 2007

It's the morning and after a good night's sleep, I'm off again. I have retraced my steps from Donnington Bridge to Folly Bridge. I took a photo of what remains of the Folly, a rather ornate, castellated building with lots of statues in lots of little niches. The Folly has been on this site apparently for 700 years. It's ten o'clock in the morning and it promises to be a very hot day. I will pack up if it gets too hot.

The Folly at Folly Bridge, Oxford

There are lots of fishermen on the south bank. I've just watched one catch a fish, a tiny little thing, not much bigger than my finger. Why do they bother? The last two fishermen have had about six rods each.

I've passed over Osney Bridge and there is a distinct change in the river. It doesn't look like a big river anymore. It's very much narrower.

A Department of the Environment boat with two uniformed officers is patrolling the river, Saturday morning. They must patrol at all times.

I'm now at Godstow Lock, having walked through a patch of land known as Port Meadow given to the people of Oxford by William the Conqueror, or King Alfred, depending on who you believe, as common land for them to use for grazing. It has a rich history: in fact, during the Civil War Charles I's army set up camp here, and the Dunkirk evacuees rested here during the Second World War.

I have been seduced, all along the way this morning, by information in my book, that there is an attractive thatched pub at Binsey called The Perch.

The Perch

An Oxford institution as old as the university.
The Perch is one of Oxford's oldest pubs. We're just a few minutes' walk from the Isis (Oxford's stretch of the Thames) and Port Meadow, a historic common stretching from Jericho to Wolvercote.

In the summer, our garden is the envy of the whole city, and our 17th-century plaster-rubble building with its traditional thatched roof will charm even the most seasoned pub-goers.

There's been a pub on our site for at least 800 years. In those 800 years, we've been a favourite of some of Britain's best poets and authors, a frequent haunt of Inspector Morse, and even an influential venue on the British jazz scene.

In spring 2015, we conducted a full-scale renovation to bring a traditional pub into the modern world, and ensure we'll be around for the next 800 years. We provide a refuge for everyone who loves great food and drink – whether they're thirsty students, hungry walkers, exploring families, muddy dogs, adventurous visitors or wedding parties.

I arrived at Binsey at a perfect time, on a hot day, only to find a notice by the track advising that The Perch was closed because new management was taking over. A major disappointment. What I didn't know, however, is that there has been an English Pope (Adrian IV), who plied his trade in the church at Binsey.

So I moved on to Plan B, which is to walk a little further to Wolvercote where The Trout pub awaits to greet a thirsty walker.

The Trout was a great stop. Adnams beer. Delicious. £2.50 per pint. The best beer I have had since I left Wycombe. Charming pub with a good food menu at reasonable prices. It was very busy but I was lucky to get a table by the riverside.

All is well with the world.

The beer garden at the Trout, Wolvercote

The Trout

The Trout Inn is a premium pub, bar, and restaurant with its very own garden, centrally located in the heart of the picturesque town of Wolvercote.

Steeped in history yet with a thoroughly contemporary twist, The Trout Inn is a 17th-century pub that provides a truly special setting to dine, drink and catch up with family and friends.

Positioned on the banks of the River Thames in Lower Wolvercote, north of Oxford, The Trout Inn is a unique British pub that provides the ultimate destination to escape the demands that come hand in hand with everyday life.

With its stylish interiors, distinctive features, and links to literary and historic greats such as Lewis Carroll, Colin Dexter's Inspector Morse,

Rosamund the Fair, and King Henry II, this pub will open your eyes to a world of fascinating history and culture.

I am suitably refreshed and rested and on my way again. My book tells me that the iron boundary marker which I am looking at was placed here in 1886 to mark the boundary of Oxford. My book describes the marker as having an ox on its top.

The authors of my book saw this and described it in their book published in 1996. The marker survived for 110 years. However, and infuriatingly, some prat has since snapped the ox off and made off with it!!

Wouldn't it be great to find the person who did it, make a large concrete replica of the ox, tie it to their ankles and throw them in the bloody river?

I'm now at Kings Lock. Another lovely Thames lock. It's just like paradise here. One or two boats moored up. One boat has put a tent up on the bank. Some have obviously permanent moorings, with lovely gardens.

I finished for the day at Eynsham Lock just upriver of Swinford Toll Bridge. I had a pint in The Talbot inn. I spoke to a chap in the pub who told me that he had set off from the source and had walked for two days before there was any water in the river.

The Talbot at Eynsham

If you're looking for a traditional village pub with a great wharfside setting, you can't do better than The Talbot at Eynsham.

The Talbot retains a traditional pub atmosphere and is a refreshing change from today's modern gastro pubs. Our menu is typical pub fayre – not too posh, not too complicated. There is a wide range of popular, tried and tested dishes and we're sure you'll find something that tickles your taste buds. But don't let its simplicity fool you.

Full of character, every corner of our pub seems to tell a story or hide a secret.

We pride ourselves on the cask ales, served directly from the barrels racked, settled and dispensed right before your eyes – no pipes and hand pulls here! We serve a great selection of hand-crafted ales from Arkell's of Swindon, expertly brewed by Alex Arkell by traditional methods passed down the generations. And I have to say, he's pretty good at it. Choose from the permanently stocked BBB or Kingsdown ale or try one of the regularly changing guest ales. This could be Wiltshire Gold, Moonlight or one of Alex's concoctions which he changes on a monthly basis to suit the season.

I got a bus back to Oxford and finished my day with another visit to The Head of the River.

The beer was excellent, but it was so very hot that I only had one, before choosing a Magners cider which I drank from a pint glass full of ice. I have one criticism of the pub. There is a huge flat-screen, very noisy TV, which was of no interest to anyone present. I asked if it could be turned off. The manager was consulted but advised that it was policy to keep it on all the bloody time.

Because of the information from the chap in the pub, I am considering perhaps one more small walk, then holding off until a wet period when the river may be more interesting.

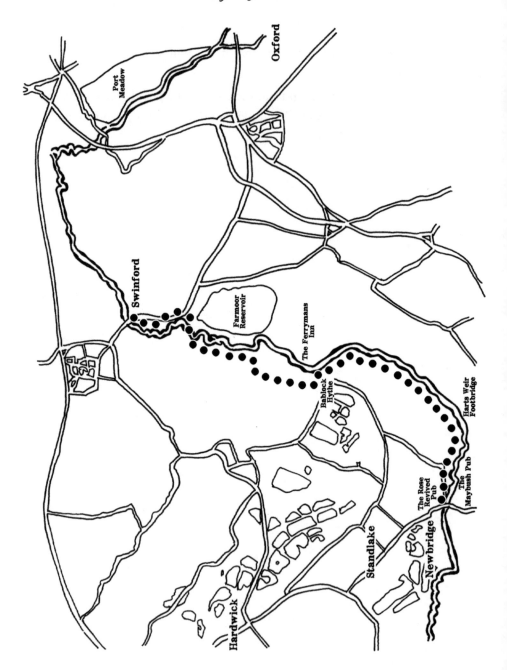

15.
Newbridge to Swinford
Friday 8 June 2007

First, a diary note – What's happening in the world?

The PM, Mr Blair, has indicated his intention to quit (a much-trailed event) and the Labour government has shoehorned that miserable Scottish man Gordon Brown into the post.

We will therefore have a PM elected by the government. We are still fighting in Afghanistan and in Iraq. Two actions that seem to be an absolute disaster.

So, what have I done today?

Well, following the last walk, which I finished at Swinford, I decided this time to camp again at Oxford and get a bus to Newbridge and walk back to Swinford.

This didn't go as well as expected.

Firstly, the journey from Oxford to Witney (where I had to change buses) took forever. A lovely ride but frustratingly long. Having arrived at Witney I found that I had just missed the bus to Newbridge and the next bus was in two hours. Two hours to kill, doing of course what comes naturally!

I visited two pubs. The first was Ye Olde Cross Keys, because I saw that they were serving Courage Best, one of my favourite beers. It was hardly fit to drink (remind me never to move to Oxfordshire).

Ye-olde-cross-keys

Charming town centre pub, large selection of gin sits alongside usual Greene King food and beverages.

I left and went to a Greene King pub, where they were serving another of my favourite beers, IPA. It was excellent.

I got a bus to Newbridge, to The Rose Revived. What a wonderful pub name. Another Greene King pub and it wouldn't be fair not to sample the IPA, for comparative purposes of course. It was delicious (£2.40, by the way).

Rose Revived

The Rose Revived pub

Ivy-covered walls, Cotswold stone, weeping willows and right on the banks of the Thames, the 16th-century Rose Revived is one of our outstanding properties. With just seven select bedrooms to choose from you're sure of a quiet stay. All cosy and welcoming, some have delightful river views. Enjoy a cask ale in front of a roaring log fire in the winter, and the sun on your face on the riverbank in our lovely garden during summer.

Although things haven't gone quite to plan, and the journeys have been long, I am pleased that I took the bus. They wander through all of the beautiful Cotswold villages, all of which are lovely. That's the thing about buses – you see and enjoy lots of places that you wouldn't normally see and the crowning glory was that the bus stop is at the pub.

It dropped me at the front door! Well, it would have been rude not to go in.

The Maybush

Pretty riverside pub across the bridge from Rose Revived, but currently closed when this book went to print in August 2019.

So these two pubs, The Maybush and Rose Revived, sit on either side of the bridge at Newbridge. During the English Civil War, the pubs were here and they witnessed skirmishes between the rival factions. To stop King Charles's blokes marching south, Cromwell's lot broke the bridge in the middle.

Apparently he had a pint in Rose Revived and this visit might have given the pub its name. It isn't clear whether he had a few beers before or after he smashed up the bridge!

Fascinating though this is, it is now two o'clock and I now have a seven-mile walk. But the world is my oyster and I have no other commitments today.

I have spoken to the management, who have said that I could leave my bicycle here for a future walk. This is good because from here, upriver, public transport is virtually non-existent.

I took photos of Rose Revived and The Maybush, which is just on the opposite side of the road.

The Maybush and the Rose Revived, sitting across "Cromwell's bridge!"

There was a bit of an odd moment this afternoon and, but for my background on farms, it could have been difficult. There was a herd of cattle, mostly laid down on the path, some stood. Some male, some female. They made no effort to move and I had to pick my way through them. Someone not used to cattle would have found that difficult to negotiate. I took some pictures.

Cattle!

There is another of those pillboxes here. I have been told that the Germans used the Thames as a navigational aid which is why these things were built all along its route.

A clump of yellow flag mirrored in the river

Here is a boat, whose owner has my sense of humour. It's called "Sick Note".

I've just been passed by a load of students who charged past and up onto a wooden footbridge (Hart's Weir Footbridge) where they proceeded to leap off into the river. What fun!

The lads that dad met jumping into the river at Hart's Weir footbridge

The house that I am looking at is a splendid house in the middle of nowhere. It must be owned by someone who is very, very rich.

The boat in the incorporated boathouse is called "The Grande Dame", which I believe is French for "Fat Lady". Why you would call a boat after a fat lady God only knows, but I'll tell you this: "The show isn't over till the Grande Dame sinks!"

I have walked for miles now, through meadows of luxurious grass and no harvesting is taking place. The grass is just being allowed to grow, ungrazed and unharvested.

It's a mystery why so much land is apparently not being used productively. It could of course be "set aside land", another example of the stupidity of Brussels. More splendid houses on the opposite bank. Must be owned by popstars.

I'm almost at Bablock Hythe, Witney, where there has been a ferry across the river for at least 1,000 years. Believe it or not, there's a canal boat moored up and a washing line, full of washing, hung between the boat and the bank.

I said, "I have to take a picture of this. Pink Knickers on Father Thames," I said. The lady said, "And they're mine." I said, "I guessed they were."

"Pink knickers on Father Thames" at Bablock Hythe, Witney

There's a pub here which has been here for as long as the ferry. It used to be called "The Chequers", but its name was changed in the 1990s to "The Ferryman Inn", for some reason. Another woman in a canal boat said the ferry wasn't running but she would take me across for £50...

The Ferryman Inn

The Ferryman Inn, situated in Witney, is a friendly public house offering a varied menu, filled with delicious options that cater to every customer's taste. Here at The Ferryman Inn, we believe in delivering an exceptional level of customer service every time; whether you're a regular visitor or a new face, you'll always be greeted with a warm welcome. Furthermore, we also offer various forms of entertainment, including charity events, discos and dances. We even have a selection of excellent facilities such as our function room, darts board and pool table. We also have a number of clean and comfortable rooms available, all competitively priced for your convenience.

Oh, and now I turn a corner and see a big meadow mown for hay. Maybe they do mow, but later than I would have expected. I've just had a treat. I heard a cuckoo.

The beer last night at "The Head of the River" was £2.80 per pint. The beer at another smaller pub, which I thought was very scruffy last time I was in Oxford, was £2.40 per pint.

It's been taken over by a young couple and they have really cleaned the place up. Apart from the kids leaping off the bridge and the pink knicker lady, I have seen no one all day. The book says that I have to make a diversion here onto the Oxford Road, because the towpath has been eroded away.

If you ask me I would say that it hasn't been eroded away, it has been nicked by these posh people in these big houses.

It's 6 o'clock. I'm at Swinford Bridge. I'm going to walk up the road, over the bridge, to find out about bus times and to hopefully find a pub. It's really hot.

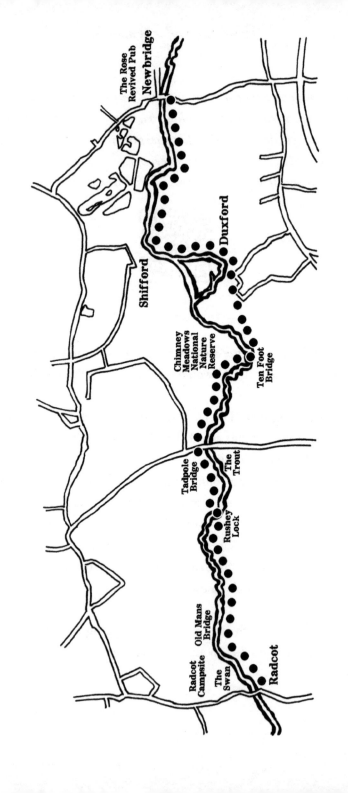

16.
Radcot to Newbridge
12 June 2008

I am beginning another section of the Thames Walk. I am at Radcot Bridge. The last stretch of the Thames that I walked finished at Newbridge, at The Rose Revived pub. I have left my bicycle at The Rose Revived and intend to walk there (about twelve miles).

At Radcot Bridge there is a pub called The Swan, which my information told me had a campsite. The pub does indeed have a campsite, but you can't really call it a campsite. It's a car park, in a field, on the opposite side of the river. It possesses no toilets or facilities of any description. The toilets, such as they are, are situated in the pub car park, over the bridge and yet, believe it or not, the overnight parking fee is £8.00. I've parked up the van and put my tent up on a tiny island on the site that is surrounded by a puddle...*

*Since Dad's visit things seem to have improved immeasurably!

Ye Olde Swan

Ye Olde Swan is situated in a stunning location aside the River Thames at Radcot Bridge, originally an old packhorse bridge on the main wool export route from Northampton to Southampton. The bridge, which claims to be the oldest crossing of the Thames, was built around 1200. Ye Olde Swan has been a stopping-off point for weary shepherds and travellers for hundreds of years to enjoy fine ales and good food. Nothing has changed, though the sheep have long since disappeared.

Ye Olde Swan has an annual music festival in July each year and (new in 2019), two unique glamping accommodations overlooking The River Thames; one is our floating accommodation, and the other is on land overlooking the tranquil waters. Both sleep up to four people. Register your interest for the Barrel Glamping Pods by emailing info@yeoldeswan.co.uk.

So what's happening in my world today? Well, personally I am a very happy man, because my daughter Jane produced a baby on Monday (8 lbs 10 oz) called Olivia. It was a difficult birth and they will be kept in hospital for a few days.

We are still fighting in Afghanistan and we are still fighting in Iraq and it's all pretty desperate. It looks likely that we will quit on Iraq soon. Some people say that we have improved things there. Some say that we have worsened them. Lots of folk think that it was a mistake to go there in the first place.

We are being ruled by a Labour government that is in my view appalling. It is just about the most undemocratic outfit that I have ever come across, except of course the EU, which is marginally less democratic than Zimbabwe under Mugabe (which, by the way, is the famous Yorkshire phrase "e ba gum" backwards).

Blair was selected as our Prime Minister until he got bored of it, quit and gave the job to a fellow called Gordon Brown who is a dour Scot and he seems to me to be a very bad choice of PM. The electorate had absolutely no say in this transfer of power. They seem to have a new idea every morning before breakfast which lasts at most until teatime, when it is ditched.

Yesterday, they got a new anti-terrorism bill through Parliament, which allows them to lock up suspects for 42 days before they are brought to trial. Most politicians seem to think that this is a poor idea, as do several senior policemen. Most of the country think it's a good idea. I agree with the cops. A black lad called Obama has won the Democratic nomination to run for President. I cannot believe that the Americans are ready yet to appoint a black President. I hope I am wrong.

*Two things to note from this passage.
1) Dad always said that it was Mum's job to look after the small things in life, such as: where we lived, where the kids went to school, what we ate, washing, drying, holidays etc, whereas it was his job to worry about the larger issues, such as world peace. Three lines on the birth of Jane's oldest and the rest on world affairs!
2) Some of these notes might make you think that Dad wasn't a Socialist. In fact he was a diehard trade unionist, shop steward, convener of civil service

strikes and a card-carrying member of the Labour Party, until Tony Blair took power, when he tore it up and posted it back to their H.Q.

The weather is rainy and cold, which is a shame after the very good spell that we have just enjoyed.

Old Radcot bridge, apparently the oldest bridge across the Thames

It's now 10 o'clock and I am off. I will walk to Tadpole Bridge (4 miles), where there is another pub where I intend to have a break and a couple of pints, then set off to Newbridge. I ought to be at Tadpole Bridge between 11 and half past. The sun is out. There is a chill in the air, the landscape is beautiful and it's a pleasure to be out in the middle of it!

Last night I had a good drink in Ye Olde Swan! I got chatting to some interesting chaps, including the landlord who had started out as an Inland Revenue tax inspector, subsequently became a tax adviser and then came across the pub.

He was advising some clients about the worthwhileness of taking it over, but at the last minute the clients pulled out. He persuaded the bank to lend him the money and he took it over. He seems to be happy with his situation! I don't suppose he makes a fortune but I don't think that he is a poor man either. Certainly a pleasant fellow to talk to, and he keeps a nice pint of beer. The beer was Greene King IPA, £2.50 for a pint and very nice indeed.

I stopped at Radcot Lock, which is some distance from Radcot, where I chatted to a man and woman who are supporting four lads who are running and rowing the Thames from Lechlade to Putney, which is a distance of 140 miles. Two run along the riverbank, whilst the other two row the river. Every so often they change roles. They are doing it for a charity.

There are lots of flowers at Radcot Lock. A splendid sight of many broadcast seeds. Presumably we have the Department of the Environment to thank for this splendid display.

Radcot Lock

"Old Man's Bridge" can also be found at Radcot Lock.

The walking here is difficult. There has been so much rain recently and the footpath is waterlogged. Fortunately there is an access road to the lock which is perfectly dry, so I am cheating a little by walking along this straight path rather than sticking to the riverbank. It is amazing how much the river meanders here. I am taking a photo to remind me of the incredible journey it makes between points that are only yards apart.

The meandering Thames

I've just had the rare pleasure of seeing a trout leap from the river. Quite a large trout, possibly 11 lbs in weight. I've just seen a little bird, I think a warbler, but I will try to properly identify it later. Strangely it carried a piece of glittery tinsel in its bill. Maybe to decorate his nest. I know that bowerbirds decorate their nests, but I've never heard of a warbler in England being so inventive. I have, however, seen many female warblers, very attractive, too. Maybe the tinsel will help him to get lucky.

It's midday. I am now at Tadpole Bridge. Half an hour later than planned but what the hell! I have taken a photo of the very lovely bridge and the pub called The Trout, with beautiful roses outside. The beer was a new one on me, "Burbury". I had a couple of pints. It was very nice, £2.60 a pint. Like many pubs on this reach of the river it was really a restaurant. The meals were very expensive, £13.00 just for lunch. Tadpole Bridge is a very pretty bridge indeed!

The Trout at Tadpole Bridge

You'll find the river meets the Cotswolds in our beautiful 17th-century inn overlooking the historic Tadpole Bridge.

Nestled deep within the Oxfordshire Cotswolds, we're a riverside inn that celebrates the very best of British country life. Surrounded by fields and with the River Thames flowing just outside our door, our menus make the most of fresh fish and local game while our cosy bar and boutique rooms are the perfect place for you to relax in classic Cotswold comfort. Whether you arrive by car, foot or even by boat, you'll always find a warm welcome here at The Trout.

The Trout

I've left the pub now. It's 1 o'clock. I am sort of on schedule. The walk to Newbridge is now six miles and at my pace that means I will get there at 3 o'clock.

Here's a thing. I am in the middle of the countryside, in the middle of nowhere. I am on my own and haven't seen a soul since I left the pub. The uncut grass is up to my knees, walking is hard and slippery because of all the rain, and here I come across a kissing gate with an attached stile. The bloody kissing gate is locked with a padlock requiring a key. There is a notice on the gate that the padlock is for disabled people who should use their special key. Why? Why lock a kissing gate? Why reserve a gate in the middle of nowhere for disabled people? Why exclude able-bodied people from using it? Is this just political correctness gone mad? I will have to climb over the bloody stile. If I had a saw on me, I would saw the lock off. Anybody who is disabled couldn't possibly have got this far. I would like a counter mounted on the gate, to see how many times a disabled person opens it each year.

It's quarter past 2. I stopped at Tenfoot Bridge.

Tenfoot Bridge was built in 1869. It connects Buckland on the south bank to Chimney on the north. The name apparently derives from a pre-existing weir which had a ten-foot-wide flash lock in it.

The river passes close to Shifford on the other bank. King Alfred held the first recorded meeting of the English Parliament at Shifford. Possibly in tents. I don't think they let him run the barbeque. The guy burnt everything.

I am here now at Newbridge, objective achieved! The second-oldest bridge over the Thames is here. Built by monks in 1250. There's a flat, well-used picnic field just before the bridge, a fairly common feature of these Thames-side villages. A place where locals and visitors can enjoy the river with minimum demands on their energy or mobility. There were two chaps of about my age sitting together in reclining chairs by two narrow boats. I got talking to them, as you do. They and their wives had departed on the canal system from Lincolnshire in April. They had boated along the canals to Nottingham. From there, via canals, they had got to the Oxford Canal and into the Thames. I think the canal enters the Thames at Shifford, and here they are. They plan to boat to Reading where they will enter the Kennet & Avon Canal, which will take them to Bristol. From there they will go to the West Country or to the South Coast. What a life!

Well, this has been the most testing part of the walk so far and has been, all day. Long grass, lots of tall nettles, deep, muddy puddles and deep water pools, with no obvious way around them. Hard work really and my boots feel like lead. But, all day, my walk has been brightened by the beautiful blue damselflies, that dip and fly and dip again. Beautiful little creatures that the newspapers tell me are in severe decline. What a privilege, then, to see them in such abundance. Thank goodness it was relatively dry. If the grass had been wet, it would have been impossible.

My last photo today is of the Maybush pub. There are two guys tidying the garden.

I will collect my bicycle for the ride back to Radcot Bridge. I am a bit knackered, so a rest and liquid refreshment seem to be in order!

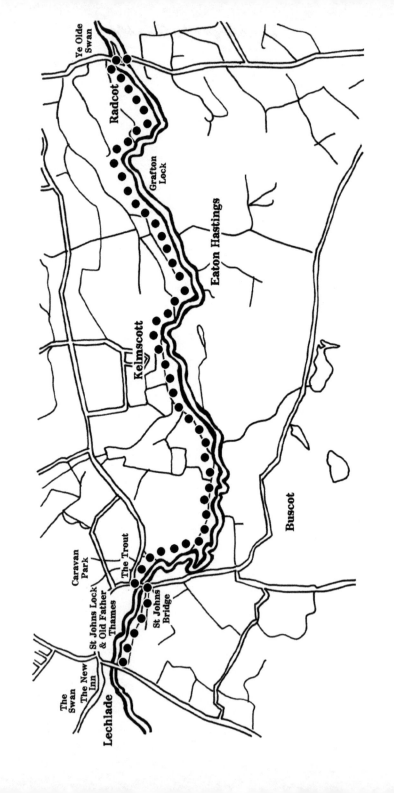

17.
Lechlade to Radcot
Saturday 14 June 2008

It's 10 o'clock. I'm all packed and ready to cycle to Lechlade. I'm booked on the campsite there tomorrow evening. I will leave my bike at the site today and walk back here to the van. It's a warm, sunny day.

Two o'clock. I've found the campsite and left my bike. I walked around Lechlade, nice little village.

I have sent a card to Simon: it's his birthday tomorrow and I've had a couple of pints in the pub by the river bridge.

The Riverside

Pretty riverside pub (and B&B), next to the bridge at Lechlade. On a hot summer's day, and especially at sunset, we don't think you can beat it. The ideal place to enjoy life with a cool drink & a bite to eat outside by the Thames.

Sitting right on the river (and where comedian David Walliams started his Sport Relief 140-mile swim down the Thames from in 2011), our garden area & terrace offers a wonderful place to watch the world go by. Looking out over the historic 18th-century Ha'penny Bridge, you'll see swans & ducks gliding past, together with boats big & small passing through or mooring up.

Those who fancy getting even closer the water can even hire a rowing boat, canoe or motor boat to enjoy a quick trip down the river to explore this wonderful part of the world some more.

My left calf muscle is hurting but I will walk despite it. I've photographed Lechlade with its magnificent church spire, from the meadow next to the campsite. If the sky is properly imagined it ought to be a "Constable" sky. I've also photographed a steer with a remarkable contraption through its nose. Must be a device to stop it suckling.

Last night, on the journey home I cycled through Brampton. I was rather hungry so I stopped at a kebab van. It was so large that I couldn't finish it.

This morning I put it into a bap and made a salad. I have just now eaten the kebab and the salad and it was delicious. Two meals out of the kebab which only cost £4.00.

I've taken pictures at St John's Lock with "Old Father Thames" on the lockside.

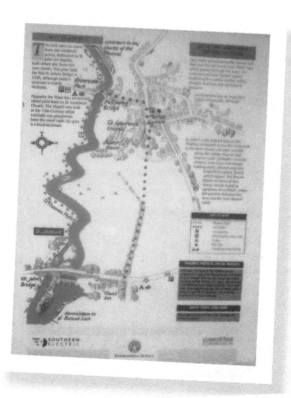

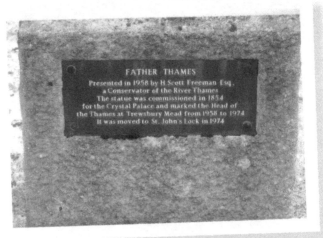

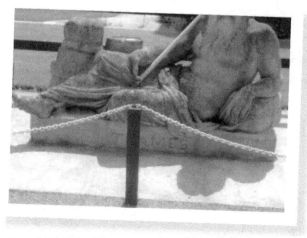

"This photo of Old Father Thames was taken with particular panache and sums the whole tale up really.....well done dad!"

I am now at Grafton Lock, only a mile or so from "home". Again, this has been hard work walking. I've taken a photo.

Nettles are three feet high and the grass is a good two feet high.

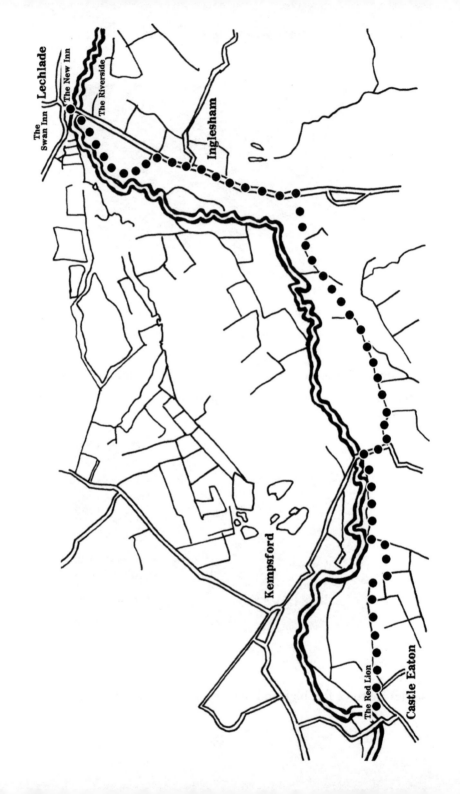

18.
Castle Eaton to Lechlade
Sunday 15 June 2008

It's Father's Day (third Sunday in June). It's also Simon's birthday.

I've had a call from Phillip and Simon wishing me, their wandering dad, a happy day. Isn't that great!?

Jane hasn't phoned yet, probably she's busy with Olivia. I'm having a lazy day. I moved camp from Radcot, to this very adequate site at Lechlade (Bridge House). Very full when I arrived but I was asked to wander off to amuse myself in the village until all the weekenders had packed up and gone.

Amusing myself in a village with several lovely pubs has never been a problem for me. I visited several, as you do on these occasions. For someone like me, Lechlade is paradise. It has two "bric-à-brac" shops which are to die for. I probably spent an hour exploring and bought some stuff.

I have booked on the site for two nights, but I so love this place I intend to stay longer.

Rainbow over Lechlade

The Trout Inn

Around 1220 the old, wooden bridge over the Thames at Lechlade was replaced by a stone one. To house the workmen entrusted with the building of it, a hospital or (almshouse) dedicated to Saint John the Baptist, was founded by Peter FitzHerbert.

In 1472, the main priory was dissolved by Edward IV, but the almshouse continued as an inn known as "Ye Sygne of St John Baptist Head" until 1704, when the name was changed to "The Trout Inn".

Ancient fishery rights granted by Royal Charter to the Brethren are still held by The Trout Inn, which controls two miles of trout and coarse fishing waters. You cannot fish directly from The Trout land these days, but the stretch of water on the south bank between the lock and Lechlade can be used during the open season, and a bailiff patrols this and collects the fees from the bank.

Over 700 years' tradition of hospitality in the provision of good food and drink is faithfully maintained today in this ancient inn.

Penny Warren has been proprietor of The Trout Inn, our proper pub in Lechlade for over 29 years, and her aim has always been to maintain The Trout Inn as a traditional English inn.

We have a riverside garden and during the summer we have a large marquee available for shelter. This, along with the Creel Bar, which is a garden bar separate from the main building, can be booked for your party or business function. During the winter months we have a roaring log fire in the main bar, which has ancient wooden beams and some stone floors.

We are not a fast-food or gastro pub, just a family-run, proper country inn with a good range of real ales, ciders, wines and spirits, all kept in a fine condition by Scott and a kitchen run with great panache by Penny.

Swan Inn

The Swan Inn is a family-run, traditional 16th-century pub in Lechlade. Debbie, Stuart and all the team offer a very warm welcome to all who visit this area on the edge of Gloucestershire, with all its country charm and atmosphere. With boats meandering along the River Thames, as well as fishing, walking, it is one of the most enchanting places in the South.

Food is served every day. The menu is varied with all dishes home-made on the premises with locally sourced ingredients where available. As the food is freshly made any changes or allergies can be accommodated where possible.

Being very dog-friendly, dogs are allowed anywhere in the bar.

New Inn Hotel

This 17th-century town centre coaching inn & hotel is an ideal setting for a stylish wedding reception, exhibition or business conference. It has a traditional bar where you can relax by the log fire. The hotel also boasts an à la carte restaurant which serves a wide variety of sumptuous dishes.

Monday 16 June 2008

I have cycled to Castle Eaton, a ten-mile bike ride. I have arrived at The Red Lion Inn, on the banks of the river.

The bike ride was not as pleasant as it should have been because of the difficulty that I am having with my left calf muscle. I had a couple of pints of Arkells £2.55 and chatted to the landlady.

She was helpful in two ways. Firstly she advised that there was a lovely campsite down the lane behind the pub. Secondly, not only did she say I could leave my bicycle there, but also she insisted on locking it up in her barn.

I have a way with widowed landladies.

The Red Lion

The Red Lion is the perfect retreat if you're looking for old and traditional village pub with high-quality fayre, and cosy log fires in winter.

In summer, The Red Lion's location means you can enjoy the English countryside by walking the Thames Path, or sitting in the pub's large garden right on the edge of the River Thames. Stop off by boat if you like!

For a family or visiting group for lunch or evening meal, the menus or snacks and refreshments certainly suit the occasion, with all-day opening on Saturdays and Sundays.

Visit or stay at this unique pub just off the A419 near Cirencester & Swindon.

Before I surrendered the bike to her charge, I cycled to the campsite. It was a lovely small site, called (hilariously) the "Second Chance Touring Park".

I spoke to a young chap who was busy doing work and turned out to be the owner. I asked why it wasn't advertised. He said that they didn't advertise. They had a regular clientele and didn't want casual punters, who may spoil the ambience. He did, however, give me his card and invited me to stay whenever I wanted, so long as there was a vacancy. (I guess there are always vacancies for "approved" tourers!)

I couldn't have looked like riff-raff, which after camping a few days in the wild was, I thought, a credit to me.

I set off at two o'clock, taking many photos of this picturesque village.

The path here is a section that doesn't follow the river. It's one of the few sections that doesn't. The walk is on lanes, until a lovely bridle path takes you down to the river bank. Amazingly, the Thames here is a tiny stream that I could almost stride across into a field on the other bank.

It seemed to be quite a river at Castle Eaton and was certainly a substantial river at Lechlade, but here it isn't a river at all. I stood in the middle in my hiking boots!

At Inglesham (does this mean 'Angels' village'?) the path leaves the river again and takes the walker on a very busy 'A' road, with virtually no verges. A bit of a nightmare. I should research to find out which selfish prat owns the riverbanks and prevents us from walking there and puts us on this unpleasant, dangerous road.

Next time it rains heavily, I will pray that his house is flooded and he has to spend days in his underpants on the roof, whilst real, worthwhile people are rescued, and the water for his gin and tonic is contaminated by raw sewage.

I also hope that his dog is ravaged by a wolf and he in turn is savaged by the offspring of the union. But I bear the man no malice. If ever there was an example of why the nation should have powers to force selfish people to share their fortune, this is one of them.

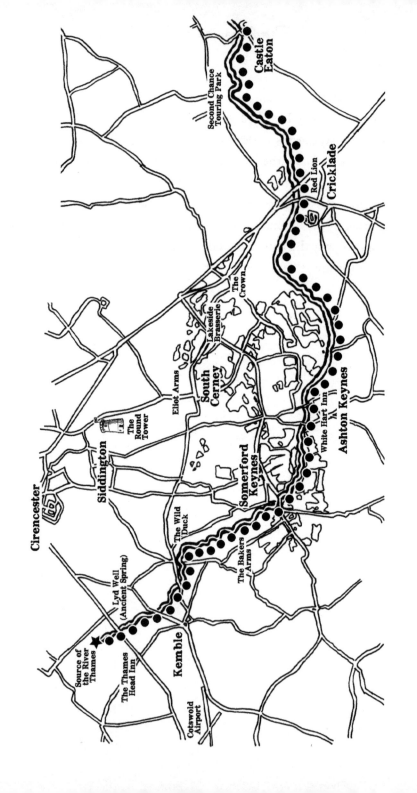

19.
Castle Eaton to the Source of the River Thames

Dad wasn't able to do this last stretch of the river, which is very sad simply because it's a beautiful walk, combining lovely Cotswolds scenery with four cracking pubs. A winning combination, that I thought I should walk in his honour.

Setting out from Castle Eaton, the river is quite hard to follow in summer months. It is always wet but very overgrown in many places. Rolling farmland on either side of the path, and occasionally some livestock to manage.

The river comes into Cricklade passing underneath the A419 and, as you enter Cricklade at the top of the High Street, you encounter The Red Lion & Hop Kettle Brewery, which is in fact a pub that hosts its own micro-brewery and boasts a huge selection of gin. It's great.

The Red Lion
Early 16th-century inn with well-liked food in two dining rooms, ten real ales, friendly, relaxed atmosphere and big garden; bedrooms.

They keep a fantastic range of drinks plus rewarding food here, and our readers also enjoy the community atmosphere and traditional décor. From their onsite Hop Kettle micro-brewery, there might be Hop Kettle C.O.B., Element and North Wall and up to seven quickly changing guests. They also keep 60 bottled beers, six farm ciders, ten wines by the glass, ten malt whiskies and 15 gins (gin hour is 5.30-6.30 pm). The bar has stools by the nice old counter, wheelbacks and other chairs around dark, wooden tables on red patterned carpet, an open fire and all sorts of bric-à-brac on the stone walls including stuffed fish, animal heads and old street signs. You can eat here or in the slightly more formal dining room, furnished with pale wooden farmhouse chairs and tables, beige carpeting and a wood-burning stove in a brick fireplace. There are plenty of picnic sets in the big back garden. Bedrooms are comfortable and breakfasts good. You can walk along the nearby Thames Path or around the historic, pretty town.

Bar food times: 12-2.30, 6.30-9; 12-2.30, 6.30-9.30 Fri, Sat; 12-3, 6.30-9 Sun

Highly thought-of food includes lunchtime sandwiches (not Sun).

The Thames Path then takes you on a pleasant walk through the Cotswold Water Park, a nature and recreational park containing more than 150 lakes, many of which were man-made by the extraction of gravel. The path follows alongside the Thames and occasionally the lakes all the way. The next stop is Ashton Keynes and the White Hart Inn.

The White Hart

A lovely Cotswold village pub, owned and managed by the locals since 2011. Our chef adapts our menu seasonally, creating consistent good, honest pub grub – with a few daily specials thrown in. Sharing boards, salads, classic burgers, and our 'whale-sized' beer-battered fish and chips, there is a little something for everyone.

Onwards from the White Hart towards Somerford Keynes. Turn right out of the pub and walk up to the top of the road. The Thames Path is marked in three different ways here: take the left-hand path, ignoring the sign to the church (unless you want to visit it). The path here continues as before, following the river and traversing the various lakes. Walk past the Lower Mill holiday home development on your left (0.7 miles to the pub from here) and then cross over the Spine Road, then head up between the houses into Somerford Keynes village: you will see The Bakers Arms on your left, just before the historic church.

The Bakers Arms

Dating back to the 17th century, The Bakers Arms is a pretty chocolate-box Cotswold pub to be found four miles south of Cirencester. Situated within the beautiful Cotswold Water Park, we are also just a short distance from the Thames Path and the Cotswold Way, making the pub a perfect watering hole to rest weary legs, enjoy a well-earned pint and spot of lunch.

We are also conveniently placed in relation to the Lower Mill Estate, from where it is a pleasant 0.7-mile stroll through Somerford Keynes village to our door.

Our cosy bar has low-beamed ceilings and an open, inglenook fireplace. In the warm weather you can enjoy your drinks and meals in one of our two spacious beer gardens. Both are secure and enclosed, one with a children's play area. Families and furry friends are welcome – this is a country pub after all.

From The Bakers Arms, turn left out of the pub, walk up the road a little way and pick up the public footpath again, on your left. You should be able to pick up the River Thames again from here and you can then follow it along the riverside, until you reach the village of Ewen.

The Wild Duck

The Wild Duck at Ewen is a must-stop place. An amazing, ancient pub with a beer garden, good selection of drinks, top-quality food & accommodation.

From The Wild Duck, follow the road towards Kemble until you pick up the footpath again. At this stage, you will need an Ordnance Survey map, as the river is hard to follow and dry for parts of the year. There is a public footpath, though, all the way to the source. Just after you cross the A429, on your right you should try to find Lyd Well, which is an ancient spring where often the very first Thames water will be gushing up from a little, grassy dell.

Cross the A433 and march up through the fields to the Thames Head memorial! Then repair to The Thames Head Inn for well-deserved refreshments…

20.
Kemble & the Source
of the Thames!

(These are Jane's notes of her trip with Dad to Kemble in April 2016)

Aware that Dad had not managed to fulfil his dream of completing his walk of the Thames Path, I thought it would be fun for myself and Molly to surprise him with a visit and a plan to go to the Head of the Thames. The plan was to drive to the most local pub, The Thames Head Inn, near Kemble, apparently a 20-minute walk to our destination, take the obligatory photo and head back for a well-earned pint.

After fighting back miraculously in the face of sepsis in October 2015, and having a pacemaker fitted at the start of 2016, Dad had a new spring in his step. We are unable to attribute this to the pacemaker or more likely to the advice given to Dad on discharge, to "put your liver on a 5/2 diet". Regardless he was a changed man. So much so that he ventured back to the Cotswolds a month later in May for a holiday and to watch the annual South Cerney "Duck Race".

I coincided our trip to the source of the Thames with one of his "5" days!

Having been brought up by a man who, having read the rest of this book, you may not believe, was always reasonable and polite, we popped into the pub to check that we could leave the car there, whilst on our expedition.

The Thames Head Inn

The Thames Head Inn is a unique Gloucestershire pub situated between the English towns of Cirencester and Tetbury serving excellent food in a friendly, relaxed atmosphere with a large, well-stocked central bar surrounded by various nooks and crannies, open fires, extensive landscaped gardens and ample car parking.

– Pub food
– Bed & breakfast
– Function room
– Caravan & camping site

The single most common topic of conversation at The Thames Head is not sport or politics, but the source of the River Thames. The pub is named after the spot, about half a mile away, where the river begins its 154-mile journey to London Bridge – or does it?

The source is disputed, though a large panel putting forward the evidence and even a statue of Old Father Thames himself show the strength of the local claim to it.

The Thames, though, is just a trickle here and it is not the river, but two other transport routes, that have put the pub on the map. Until Dr Beeching wielded his axe to the railways in the 1960s, the pub was next door to Tetbury Road station and with that gone, the car now brings almost all visitors to its doors. Otherwise it is a rather isolated spot.

This is a welcoming pub renowned for its good food and it has an attractive layout with a large, central bar surrounded by various nooks and crannies and a non-smoking area.

For staying longer, The Thames Head offers four beautifully decorated rooms in a barn conversion at the rear of the pub. All of the rooms are en suite with TVs, tea- & coffee-making facilities and their own individual Wi-Fi hotspot. For those who like to take their accommodation with them, there is a newly completed caravan and camping site to the rear of the pub.

I explained to the landlady our plan and as she peered around me and Molly's buggy, and looking at Dad, she said, "You're planning to do what?" Her face said it all. At this point I should have realised there was a flaw in my plan, however hindsight is all well and good. Although bemused with my plan, she was very helpful and explained that you turn left out of the pub car park, walk down the road, left again along the rail track, cross the rail track, into the fields and it is somewhere down there.

So off we went. Needless to say we got about three minutes into our 20-minute walk and Dad stopped for a rest. He then walked for another minute and a half and stopped for a rest. He then walked for another two minutes and then stopped. He was done.

Fortunately I had a cunning plan and a buggy. I persuaded Molly to get out and Dad to get into the buggy. Don't ever try this, buggies are not made for adults and it would not move. Not only does a buggy not move when an adult is sitting in it, but it's also surprisingly difficult to get an adult out of a buggy. Particularly an adult who struggles to put weight on his legs. In the end I had to tip Dad from the buggy, a bit like how you tip dirt from a wheelbarrow.

A decision was made for me and Molly to go on a recce to the end of the path and across the railway track, to the field, to see how far away the Head of the Thames actually was. You can't see the Head of the Thames from this viewpoint, which is probably about a ten-minute walk from the pub. Having since been to the Head of the Thames, it is probably a 20-minute walk from this point, if you are a professional speedwalker.

We made our way back to Dad, with heavy heart, aware there was absolutely no hope of Dad making the journey and as he asked, "How much further?" I probably felt like he did when we used to ask the same question on our way to see his family in Preston, as we passed Oxford and then every 20 minutes for the next 170 miles.

Positive as ever, he didn't let his disappointment show, was pleased we had managed to get him out of the buggy and suggested it was time for a pint. We made our way back to the pub slowly, to be met by the lovely landlady, who enthusiastically asked, "Had we made it?" No, not this time…

I promised Dad that I would take him back the following month, with the wheelchair and another pair of hands, and he would see the Head of the Thames.

Sadly, this wasn't to be. Dad passed away two months later on 22 June 2016.

Five months after this visit, Phillip, Simon and I and all of Dad's grandchildren successfully made it to the Head of the Thames with Dad's ashes

Epilogue

I am conscious that such a jolly tale has ended on a sad note.

In an ideal world my dad would have lived forever, telling his gags, drinking his beer, and making friends wherever he went. At the end of May 2016, dad stayed at our Cotswolds house for a week. He made such good mates with the locals in the pubs of the village that when it was time to leave our house, he checked into the Eliot Arms in South Cerney instead and stayed for a few more days, staying to watch the world famous Duck Race on Bank Holiday Monday!

However, all good things must come to an end at some stage, so this book has been written for you all to record his 184-mile, beer-tasting adventure, along the Thames Path National Trail from the flood barrier at Charlton to the source near Kemble. And that is certainly something worth remembering and celebrating.

When someone has gone, what do people say? "Smile and remember the good times."

Well in this case…..EASY PEASY! And so as I said in the introduction of this book, if this story transports you back a few years to some happy memories, or even if you just want to know what sort of bloke my dad was, then every second that I have spent preparing this book for you all will have been very worthwhile. One of my dad's favourite songs was "Everything Possible" by Roy Bailey, a real theme tune for my dad's life. He believed that we can achieve whatever we set our minds to in life and so here we are, together we have written a book. Who would have thought it!

And …….. if at some stage over the next few decades, just a handful of people do parts of the walk and stop at one of the pubs and raise a glass to my dad, wouldn't that be magnificent?

Love you Dad x

As he said when he made a toast with his pint, "After all, we owe it to the kids, don't we?"

Dad at Xmas… probably in full flow singing "The 12 days of Christmas"… "oh no he wasn't, oh yes he probably was…"

Dad's twin brother Jim and oldest brother Tony

My brother Simon and Dad

Dad with his sister Margaret